# A GREAT AND
# GOOD MAN

## George Washington

Before attending the morning sessions of the Constitutional Convention on 3, 6, and 9 July 1787, George Washington sat for a portrait by Charles Willson Peale. Peale used this painting to create a mezzotint print that he advertised for sale in mid-September. Here reproduced is a proof of this print from The Metropolitan Museum of Art in New York City, Bequest of Charles Allen Munn, 1924. [24.90.185]

The portrait of Washington on the dust jacket, a copy of Peale's original portrait, was painted around 1788 by James Peale, Charles' brother. It is in the collection of the New York Public Library, Astor, Lenox and Tilden Foundations.

# A GREAT AND GOOD MAN

## George Washington
## in the Eyes of His Contemporaries

꽃 꽃

*Edited by*
JOHN P. KAMINSKI AND JILL ADAIR McCAUGHAN

*Sponsored by*
The Center for the Study of the American Constitution
The New York Commission on the Bicentennial of
the United States Constitution
The Virginia Commission on the Bicentennial
of the United States Constitution

ROWMAN & LITTLEFIELD PUBLISHERS, INC.
*Lanham • Boulder • New York • Toronto • Plymouth, UK*

ROWMAN & LITTLEFIELD PUBLISHERS, INC.

Published in the United States of America
by Rowman & Littlefield Publishers, Inc.
A wholly owned subsidiary of The Rowman & Littlefield Publishing Group, Inc.
4501 Forbes Boulevard, Suite 200, Lanham, Maryland 20706
www.rowmanlittlefield.com

Estover Road
Plymouth PL6 7PY
United Kingdom

Distributed by National Book Network

British Library Cataloguing in Publication Information Available

**Library of Congress Cataloging-in-Publication Data**

The hardback edition of this book was previously cataloged by the Library of Congress as
follows:

A Great and good man.
Includes index.
1. Washington, George, 1732–1799. 2. Presidents—United States—Biography. I.
Kaminski, John P. II. McCaughan, Jill Adair, 1968– . III. University of Wisconsin–
Madison. Center for the Study of the American Constitution. IV. New York State
Commission on the Bicentennial of the United States Constitution. V. Virginia
Commission on the Bicentennial of the United States Constitution.
E312.62.G63 1989
973.4'1'0924 [B]                                        89-2547

ISBN-13: 978-0-945612-10-0 (cloth : alk. paper)
ISBN-10: 0-945612-10-9 (cloth : alk. paper)
ISBN-13: 978-0-7425-5943-1 (pbk. : alk. paper)
ISBN-10: 0-7425-5943-2 (pbk. : alk. paper)

Printed in the United States of America

♾™ The paper used in this publication meets the minimum requirements of American
National Standard for Information Sciences—Permanence of Paper for Printed Library
Materials, ANSI/NISO Z39.48-1992.

# CONTENTS

# PREFACE

GEORGE WASHINGTON STARTED his adult life like many other of the rising gentry in mid-eighteenth-century Virginia. It was his fate to live in an extraordinary time. The American Revolutionary Era gave talented men of middling circumstances an opportunity to reach previously unexpected heights.

In accepting the command of the American forces in 1775, Washington was thrust into a perilous position. Throughout the long, eight-year war, Washington repeatedly demonstrated his leadership ability. He, more than any other individual, kept the war effort alive through difficult times, and he did so without sacrificing the principles Americans cherished.

During and after the war, Washington became a symbol for the country. After his death, the man and the symbol became subservient to Washington the myth—the cherry-tree chopper and the dollar thrower. Unfortunately, too many Americans know only this mythical Washington. Recent attempts to demystify Washington destroy the legends but fail to restore the man and his true achievements. These studies are often based on superficial research arranged to suit some predetermined thesis. As more and more of the volumes of *The Papers of George Washington* are published by the University Press of Virginia, the true Washington will be recognized. In the meantime, *A Great and Good Man* attempts to make available—both to scholars and to the general public—some of the most important original documents that deal with Washington's career and reputation. Especially revealing are the many newspaper essays and poems which have never been republished since their original printings 200 years ago. It is hoped that Americans will once again appreciate how important Washington was to the Revolutionary generation that gave us Independence and the Constitution. When his contemporaries called him "The Father of His Country," they did so with gratitude and love. His dual legacy was revered 200 years ago and this book is intended to help modern readers understand why.

\*    \*

The documents in this volume have been transcribed verbatim from the original sources. No punctuation has been added and misspellings have not been corrected except for obvious typographical errors. Footnotes provided by the original authors have been marked with asterisks and appear at the bottom of the page.

\*    \*

The editors wish to acknowledge a number of people who assisted in the development of this book. Drs. W.W. Abbot, Timothy G. O'Rourke, and Stephen L. Schechter offered early encouragement when asked about the feasibility of such a book. Richard Leffler, deputy director of The Center for the Study of the American Constitution, reviewed the introductory material and almost daily served as a sounding board in the evolution of the volume. Jeremy Downes contributed both his advice and support. Paula Pfannes transcribed most of the documents, and Charles D. Hagermann encoded the manuscript for computer typesetting.

# FOREWORD

A NUMBER OF THINGS stand out in this wonderful collection of writings bearing on American efforts to form and maintain a firmer union following the winning of independence from Britain in 1783. In a sense, Washington kicked off the campaign to strengthen or replace the Articles of Confederation, our first federal instrument of government, convinced that it could not meet the needs of the post-war nation. He did so in his circular letter to the Executives of the States, as he waited impatiently for the final treaty of peace to be signed in Paris. It is a most appropriate document to begin this volume, for the general reflected on the dangers of disunity and the need for a more cohesive political system. His letters here reveal that he was probably more convinced of the serious state of affairs than any of his countrymen. Certainly his frank and open commentaries on the subject were as crucial as anything in inspiring other prominent political figures, including some of his most devoted correspondents—James Madison, Henry Knox, and Gouverneur Morris—to spearhead the movement for what became the Constitutional Convention in Philadelphia. His hesitancy about attending that gathering in 1787 because of his having already declined to preside over the triennial meeting of the Society of the Cincinnati in that same city could not, after much deliberation, keep him from participating.

So too his having served as the president of the Constitutional Convention and his support of the new parchment during the Ratification struggle meant that he could not decline to accept the presidency in 1789. Indeed, as this volume illustrates, between 1786 and 1789 he received a barrage of letters, newspaper essays, and poems affirming that the fate of America rested in his hands. All that was intense pressure unlike that experienced by any other man in the history of American public life.

Washington was a remarkably open and honest man. With him, what you saw was what you got. He really did not want to attend the Constitutional Convention or accept the presidency. He hardly spoke an untruth about being weary of public life as he reached his late fifties. He knew that his male Washington ancestors had all entered their graves in the old Bridges Creek Cemetery before reaching his age. He had already served America as commander in chief of the Revolutionary Continental Army for the eight-and-a-half-year duration of the struggle with Britain; and he did so without a single leave of absence, surely a record for continuous active duty unequalled in our military history. Even so, he never completely closed the door on the Philadelphia convention or on the presidency. He left it ajar, willing to reverse himself only if his denials would be interpreted as irresponsible conduct when his countrymen were again in dire need of his services.

If his countrymen were euphoric that Washington had agreed to become the first president, prompting an outburst of poetry about their hero, the chief executive voiced sober thoughts about their flattering but unrealistic expectations of him or of any other human being ever bestowed with such "Effusions of Gratitude," past or present. A modest man, he nevertheless realized that as the leader of the Revolution and as the nation's initial president, he had enormous symbolic significance. He needed to be visible. Consequently, between 1789 and 1791 he visited every state in the union so that he could demonstrate his interest in his countrymen and learn their opinions on the problems that confronted the infant republic. In 1792, he again faced a decision about whether to remain in public service by accepting a second term as president. Once more, he bowed to the national will, after initially asking Congressman James Madison to draft a farewell message. Four years later in 1796, somewhat bruised and battered by the onset of political party warfare and a dangerous foreign policy crisis with Great Britain, he insisted on stepping down from office, and Americans were now willing to see him take his well-earned retirement. Before leaving, he brought forth his Farewell Address, a revised and expanded document that drew partly on Madison's draft of four years earlier.

The editors of this well-crafted volume are to be commended, and this new paperback edition of *A Great and Good Man* brings to our attention the remarkable character and momentous influence of this nation's first president. The documents gathered here will continue to make timely reading for all those Americans who wish to better understand the American Founding and the role of Washington in bringing that era to fruition.

R. Don Higginbotham
Dowd Professor of History
The University of North Carolina at Chapel Hill

# INTRODUCTION

GEORGE WASHINGTON ENTERED the Revolution a prominent Virginian, but emerged from it a great and good man. Throughout the war, Washington had demonstrated his leadership abilities. As commander in chief, he could not afford the luxury of daring battlefield tactics. The General carefully had to choose his encounters with the enemy—his army had to live to fight another day if independence were to be won. During the war his tactics aroused much controversy, but, with the victory at Yorktown in April 1781, Washington's military prowess was unchallenged.

The events of 1783, however, ensured Washington a special place in history. In March of that year, disgruntled American army officers at Washington's headquarters at Newburgh, N.Y., planned to threaten Congress with the power of the army if promises of postwar pensions were not kept. Washington adroitly defused the situation while promising to lobby Congress on the officers' behalf. Three months later, the commander in chief, fulfilling a promise he had made eight years earlier in an address to the New York legislature, sent a circular to the state executives announcing that he was ready to retire to private life, never again to return to public service. When the last of the British troops evacuated New York City in late November 1783, Washington began a month-long series of good-byes that culminated in the surrender of his commission to Congress in Annapolis on 23 December. Comparisons immediately arose with the legendary Cincinnatus who had been called from his farm to save Rome and then retired to rural life. Here, in modern times—in America—a real Cincinnatus lived. Washington's resignation elevated him to a new level of republican virtue. Thomas Jefferson echoed the opinion of most Americans when he told the General that he had "prevented this revolution from being closed, as most others have been, by a subversion of that liberty it was intended to establish." This was truly a great and good man.

Three years later, with the country in the throes of a severe postwar economic depression that threatened social and political chaos, the American Cincinnatus was called out of retirement. His willingness to serve in the Virginia delegation to the Constitutional Convention and his election as president of that body instilled faith in the American people that the delegates meeting in Philadelphia could be trusted and that whatever they proposed would benefit America. Americans were confident that General Washington—with fellow delegate Benjamin Franklin, the only other American on the same plane as Washington—would not allow the Convention to propose measures destructive of the revolutionary principles so dearly purchased with American blood.

With the adoption of the Constitution, Americans realized that Washington was the only man who could successfully implement the new government as president. On the eve of the inauguration, a correspondent in the *Gazette of the United States* reported the astonishing fact that, if every individual were "*personally* consulted as to the man whom they would elect to fill the office of PRESIDENT," every voice would be raised for Washington. Philadelphia printer Mathew Carey expressed the opinion of most Americans that "Nothing but the advancement of the illustrious Washington to the head of the administration of our govt. could have so thoroughly reconciled all ranks of people to it. The govt. now fully possesses the Confidence of the people." This confidence was vividly demonstrated as the President travelled northward for his inauguration and as he toured every state during his first term of office. The affection for him personally and the respect for the new government he represented bode well for the new experiment. The great and good Washington had renewed the people's faith in themselves and in their new government.

George Washington left an important legacy for the American people. Largely through his efforts a new federal Constitution was drafted and ratified. Washington, as the first President, molded that Constitution into an energetic national government that protected the interests of the states and the rights of the people. Throughout his career, Washington demonstrated that government ought to be the protector of the people— not solely their ruler. Through his consistent subordination of the military to the civil authorities, his support for a bill of rights, his precedent-setting two-term presidency, and his unflagging belief that governmental officials ought strictly to adhere to the laws of the land, George Washington established an example Americans have been trying to emulate for 200 years.

* *

The appellation "a great and good man" possibly originated with Joseph Addison's *The Campaign* (1704, lines 219–22), a poem that lauded the Duke of Marlborough's victory over the French and Bavarian armies at Blenheim in 1704. Marlborough was described as:

"Unbounded courage and compassion join'd,
   Temp'ring each other in the victor's mind,
   Alternately proclaim him good and great,
   And make the hero and the man compleat."

# I

## THE LEGACY

### *General Washington's Parting Advice*

B<small>Y</small> 1783, <small>THE</small> W<small>AR FOR</small> I<small>NDEPENDENCE</small> had been won and the American Commander in Chief waited anxiously for the definitive peace treaty. Although hostilities had ended, Washington realized that he sat on a powder keg. He could not disband the army, for fear that the British would resume the conflict. At the same time, he knew that the disgruntled army sat around waiting to be mustered out of the service, angry that Congress had not paid the soldiers' back pay and that it probably would not honor postwar pensions for officers agreed to when times were desperate. The situation became explosive in March 1783 when, at Washington's headquarters in Newburgh, New York, a number of officers plotted to blackmail Congress into meeting its commitments. Force was even threatened. Washington, however, deftly stifled the conspiracy as he promised to intercede for the officers.

Even before the Newburgh Conspiracy, Washington had thought about writing a farewell address. Throughout the war years and after, Washington had advocated granting Congress more power. A farewell address would allow him the opportunity to put forth the plea of the officers while also recommending that the states cede some authority to Congress. Superintendent of Finance Robert Morris and Alexander Hamilton wrote the General asking him to use his "exertions" that were as necessary "to perpetuate our union" as they had been to achieve independence. In responding to Morris on 3 June, Washington wrote that "before I retire . . . I shall with the greatest freedom give my sentiments to the States on several political subjects." Within a week, Washington had written his circular letter to the state executives. Copies were sent to all of the governors by 21 June.

Washington's circular letter emphasized four things to assure the continued existence of the United States as a sovereign entity. The powers of Congress had to be increased, the war debt had to be paid, the state militias had to be standardized, and the states had to abandon "local prejudices and policies." At the end of the letter, Washington asked the governors to communicate his sentiments to their legislatures. He then announced that he would permanently retire from public service and that the recommendations in his letter should be considered his legacy to his country.

The reaction to Washington's letter was staggering. Governors and legislatures heaped praise on the retiring General, who had won "the invaluable Prize" of independence from the mightiest nation in the world. Unlike most other military figures, however, Washington was also honored because throughout the war, he had not "encroached upon the civil power" of Congress. Despite the sufferings and privations of the army, often due to the failure of the states and Congress to offer timely support, the Commander in Chief had never "used the sword to supply . . . necessities." Now, at the height of his power, when voices were repeatedly raised suggesting that Washington should be crowned king, the General chose to retire to Mount Vernon never more to hold public office. This was truly a unique man—a great *and* good man, who was uncorrupted by power.

Washington's circular letter was widely reprinted in newspapers and as pamphlets. As the postwar depression and the political turmoil of 1785–86 shattered the euphoria of the newly independent country, Washington's letter was re-examined for clues as to why the American experiment seemed not to be working. On the eve of the Constitutional Convention, the Providence *United States Chronicle*, 15 March 1787, reprinted the General's letter with a brief introduction: "At this Time, when the Anxiety of every Friend to America is excited, by the Troubles existing throughout the Union; and when a Convention is forming, with the express Intention of altering the Confederation, perhaps a Republication of the following LETTER, from one of the best Friends America ever had, may not be deemed amiss:—Had our Countrymen attended to the Advice contained therein, it is more than probable, we should now have been a united and a happy People;—but, perhaps, it is not yet too late, if proper Measures are taken to give the Federal Government due Energy, America may yet convince the World, that the favorite Maxim of Tyrants, '*That Mankind are not made to be free*,' is without Foundation."

The text of the circular letter is taken from this printing of the *U.S. Chronicle*.

# *Advice to the States*

GEORGE WASHINGTON TO THE
EXECUTIVES OF THE STATES, JUNE 1783

SIR, The great object for which I had the honor to hold an appointment in the service of my country, being accomplished, I am now preparing to resign it into the hands of Congress, and return to that domestic retirement, which, it is well known, I left with the greatest reluctance; a retirement for which I have never ceased to sigh through a long and painful absence, in which (remote from the noise and trouble of the world) I meditate to pass the remainder of life, in a state of undisturbed repose: But, before I carry this resolution into effect, I think it a duty incumbent on me to make this my last official communication, to congratulate you on the glorious events which Heaven has been pleased to produce in our favour, to offer my sentiments respecting some important subjects, which appear to me to be intimately connected with the tranquility of the United States, to take my leave of your Excellency as a public character, and to give my final blessing to that country, in whose service I have spent the prime of my life; for whose sake I have consumed so many anxious days and watchful nights, and whose happiness, being extremely dear to me, will always constitute no inconsiderable part of my own.

Impressed with the liveliest sensibility on this pleasing occasion, I will claim the indulgence of dilating the more copiously on the subject of our mutual felicitation. When we consider the magnitude of the prize we contended for, the doubtful nature of the contest, and the favourable manner in which it has terminated, we shall find the greatest possible reason for

4

gratitude and rejoicing: This is a theme that will afford infinite delight to every benevolent and liberal mind, whether the event in contemplation be considered as the source of present enjoyment, or the parent of future happiness; and we shall have equal occasion to felicitate ourselves on the lot which Providence has assigned us, whether we view it in a natural, a political, or moral point of light.

The citizens of America, placed in the most enviable condition, as the sole lords and proprietors of a vast tract of continent, comprehending all the various soils and climates of the world, and abounding with all the necessaries and conveniences of life, are now, by the late satisfactory pacification, acknowledged to be possessed of absolute freedom and independency; they are from this period to be considered as the actors on a most conspicuous theatre, which seems to be peculiarly designated by Providence for the display of human greatness and felicity: Here they are not only surrounded with every thing that can contribute to the completion of private and domestic enjoyment, but Heaven has crowned all its other blessings by giving a surer opportunity for political happiness, than any other nation has ever been favored with. Nothing can illustrate these observations more forcibly than a recollection of the happy conjuncture of times and circumstances, under which our Republic assumed its rank among the Nations. The foundation of our empire was not laid in the gloomy age of ignorance and superstition, but at an epocha when the rights of mankind were better understood and more clearly defined, than at any former period: Researches of the human mind after social happiness have been carried to a great extent: The treasures of knowledge acquired by the labours of philosophers, sages and legislators, through a long succession of years, are laid open for use, and their collected wisdom may be happily applied in the establishment of our forms of government: The free cultivation of letters: The unbounded extension of commerce: The progressive refinement of manners: The growing liberality of sentiment, and, above all, the pure and benign light of Revelation, have had a meliorating influence on mankind, and encreased the blessings of society. At this auspicious period the United States came into existence as a Nation, and if their citizens should not be completely free and happy, the fault will be entirely their own.

Such is our situation, and such are our prospects; but notwithstanding the cup of blessing is thus reached out to us, notwithstanding happiness is ours, if we have a disposition to seize the occasion and make it our own; yet it appears to me, there is an option still left to the United States of America, whether they will be respectable and prosperous, or contemptible and miserable as a nation: This is the time of their political probation; this is the moment, when the eyes of the whole world are turned upon them, this is the moment to establish or ruin their national character forever; this is the favorable moment to give such a tone to the federal government, as will enable it to answer the ends of its institution; or this may be the ill-fated moment for relaxing the powers of the union, annihilating the cement of the confederation, and exposing us to become the sport of European politics, which may play one State against another, to prevent their growing importance, and to serve their own interested purposes. For, according to the system of policy the States shall adopt at this moment, they will stand or fall; and, by their conformation or lapse, it is yet to be decided, whether the revolution must ultimately be considered as a blessing or a curse; not to the present age alone, for with our fate will the destiny of unborn millions be involved.

With this conviction of the importance of the present crisis, silence in me would be a crime; I will therefore speak to your Excellency the language of freedom and of sincerity, without disguise. I am aware, however, those who differ from me in political sentiments may, perhaps, remark, I am stepping out of the proper line of my duty; and may possibly ascribe to arrogance or ostentation, what I know is alone the result of the purest intention; but the rectitude of my own heart, which disdains such unworthy motives; the part I have hitherto acted in life, the determination I have formed of not taking any share in public business hereafter; the ardent desire I feel and shall continue to manifest, of quietly enjoying in private life, after all the toils of war, the benefits of a wise and liberal government, will, I flatter myself, sooner or later, convince my countrymen that I could have no sinister views in delivering with so little reserve the opinions contained in this address.

There are four things which I humbly conceive are essential to the well-being, I may even venture to say, to the existence of the United States as an independent power.

1st. An indissoluble Union of the States under one Federal Head.

2dly. A sacred regard to Public Justice.

3dly. The adoption of a proper Peace-Establishment. And,

4thly. The prevalence of that pacific and friendly disposition among the people of the United States, which will induce them to forget their local prejudices and policies, to make those mutual concessions which are requisite to the general prosperity, and, in some instances, to sacrifice their individual advantages to the interest of the community.

These are the pillars on which the glorious fabric of our independency and national character must be supported.—Liberty is the basis,—and whoever should dare to sap the foundation or overturn the structure, under whatever specious pretexts he may attempt it, will merit the bitterest execrations, and the severest punishment, which can be inflicted by his injured country.

On the three first articles I will make a few observations; leaving the last to the good sense, and serious consideration of those immediately concerned.

Under the first head, although it may not be necessary or proper for me in this place to enter into a particular disquisition of the principles of the Union, and to take up the great question which has been frequently agitated, whether it be expedient and requisite for the States to delegate a larger proportion of power to Congress, or not; yet it will be a part of my duty, and that of every true patriot to assert, without reserve, and to insist upon the following positions.—That unless the States will suffer Congress to exercise those prerogatives they are undoubtedly invested with by the constitution, every thing must very rapidly tend to anarchy and confusion. That it is indispensable to the happiness of the individual States, that there should be lodged, somewhere, a supreme power, to regulate and govern the general concerns of the confederated republic, without which the Union cannot be of long duration.

That there must be a faithful and pointed compliance on the part of every State with the late proposals and demands of Congress, or the most fatal consequences will ensue.—That whatever measures have a tendency to dissolve the Union, or contribute to violate or lessen the sovereign authority, ought to be considered as hostile to the liberty and independency of America, and the authors of them treated accordingly.— And lastly, that unless we can be enabled by the concurrence of the States to participate of the fruits of the revolution and enjoy the essential benefits of civil society, under a form of government so free, and uncorrupted, so happily guarded against the danger of oppression, as has been devised and adopted by the Articles of Confederation, it will be a subject of regret, that so much blood and treasure have been lavished for no purpose; that so many sufferings have been encountered without a compensation, and that so many sacrifices have been made in vain. Many other considerations might here be adduced to prove, that without an entire conformity to the spirit of the Union, we cannot exist as an independent power. It will be sufficient for my purpose to mention but one or two, which seem to me of the greatest importance. It is only in our united character, as an empire, that our independence is acknowledged, that our power can be regarded, or our credit supported among foreign nations. The treaties of the European powers, with the United States of America, will have no validity on a dissolution of the Union. We shall be left nearly in a state of nature, or we may find by our own unhappy experience, that there is a natural and necessary progression from the extreme of anarchy to the extreme of tyranny; and that arbitrary power is most easily established on the ruins of liberty abused to licentiousness.

As to the second article, which respects the performance of public justice, Congress have, in their late address to the United States, almost exhausted the subject; they have explained their ideas so fully, and have enforced the obligations the States are under to render complete justice to all the public creditors, with so much dignity and energy, that, in my opinion, no real friend to the honour and independency of America can hesitate a single moment respecting the propriety of complying with the just and honourable measures proposed; if their arguments do not produce conviction, I know of nothing that will have greater influence, especially when we recollect that the system referred to, being the result of the collected wisdom of the continent, must be esteemed, if not perfect, certainly the least objectionable of any that could be devised; and that, if it shall not be carried into immediate execution, a national bankruptcy, with all its deplorable consequences, will take place before any different plan can possibly be proposed or adopted; so pressing are the present circumstances, and such is the alternative now offered to the States.

The ability of the country to discharge the debts, which have been incurred in its defence, is not to be doubted: An inclination, I flatter myself, will not be wanting; the path of our duty is plain before us: Honesty will be found, on every experiment, to be the best and only true policy. Let us then, as a nation, be just; let us fulfil the public contracts which Congress had undoubtedly a right to make for the purpose of carrying on the war, with the same good faith we suppose ourselves bound to perform our private engagements. In the mean time let an attention to the cheerful performance of their proper business, as individuals, and as members of society, be earnestly inculcated on the citizens of America; then will they strengthen the hands of government, and be happy under its protection. Every one will reap the fruit of his labours: Every one will enjoy his own acquisitions, without molestation and without danger.

In this state of absolute freedom and perfect security, who will grudge to yield a very little of his property to support the common interests of society, and ensure the protection of government? Who does not remember the frequent declarations at the commencement of the war, that we should be completely satisfied, if at the expence of one half, we could defend the remainder of our possessions? Where is the man to be found, who wishes to remain indebted for the defence of his own person and property to the exertions, the bravery and the blood of others, without making one generous effort to repay the debt of honour and of gratitude? In what part of the Continent shall we find any man, or body of men, who would not blush to stand up and propose measures purposely calculated to rob the soldier of his stipend, and the public creditor of his due? And were it possible, that such a flagrant instance of injustice could ever happen, would it not excite the general indignation, and tend to bring down, upon the authors of such measures, the aggravated vengeance of Heaven? If, after all, a spirit of disunion, or a temper of obstinacy and perverseness should manifest itself in any of the States; if such an ungracious disposition should attempt to frustrate all the happy effects that might be expected to flow from the Union; if there should be a refusal to comply with the requisitions for funds to discharge the annual interest of the public debts, and if that refusal should revive again all those jealousies and produce all those evils which are now happily removed: Congress, who have in all their transactions shewn a great degree of magnanimity and justice, will stand justified in the sight of God and man! And that State alone, which puts itself in opposition to the aggregate wisdom of the continent, and follows such mistaken and pernicious councils, will be responsible for all the consequences.

For my own part, conscious of having acted, while a servant of the public, in the manner I conceived best suited to promote the real interests of my country; having, in consequence of my fixed belief, in some measure, pledged myself to the army, that their country would finally do them complete and ample justice; and not wishing to conceal any instance of my official conduct from the eyes of the world, I have thought proper to transmit to your Excellency the enclosed collection of papers, relative to the half-pay and commutation granted by Congress, to the officers of the army; from these communications, my decided sentiment will be clearly comprehended, together with the conclusive reasons which induced me, at an early period, to recommend the adoption of this measure in the most earnest and serious manner. As the proceedings of Congress, the Army, and myself, are open to all, and contain in my opinion sufficient information to remove the prejudices and errors which may have been entertained by any, I think it unnecessary to say any thing more, than just to observe, that the resolutions of Congress, now alluded to, are as undoubtedly and absolutely binding upon the United States, as the most solemn acts of confederation or legislation.

As to the idea, which I am informed has in some instances prevailed, that the half-pay and commutation are to be regarded merely in the odious light of a pension, it ought to be exploded forever: That provision should be viewed, as it really was, a reasonable compensation offered by Congress, at a time when they had nothing else to give to the officers of the army, for services then to be performed: It was the only means to prevent a total dereliction of the service: It was a part of their hire, I may be allowed to say, it was the price of their blood, and of your independency; it is therefore more than a common debt, it is a debt of honour; it can never be considered as a pension, or gratuity, nor cancelled until it is fairly discharged.

With regard to the distinction between officers and soldiers, it is sufficient, that the uniform experience of every nation of the world, combined with our own, proves the utility and propriety of the discrimination. Rewards in proportion to the aids the public draws from them are unquestionably due to all its servants. In some lines the soldiers have perhaps generally had as ample compensation for their services, by the large bounties which have been paid to them, as their officers will receive in the proposed commutation; in others, if, besides the donation of land, the payment of arrearages of cloathing and wages (in which articles all the component parts of the army must be put upon the same footing) we take into the estimate, the bounties many of the soldiers have received, and the gratuity of one year's full pay, which is promised to all, possibly their situation (every circumstance being duly considered) will not be deemed less eligible than that of the officers.

Should a further reward, however, be judged equitable, I will venture to assert, no man will enjoy greater satisfaction than myself in seeing an exemption from taxes for a limited time (which has been petitioned for in some instances) or any other adequate immunity or compensation granted to the brave defenders of their country's cause: But neither the adoption nor rejection of this proposition will, in any manner, affect, much less militate against, the act of Congress, by which they have offered five years full pay, in lieu of the half-pay for life, which had been before promised to the officers of the army.

Before I conclude the subject of public justice, I cannot omit to mention the obligations this country is under to that meritorious class of veterans, the non-commissioned officers and privates, who have been discharged for inability, in consequence of the resolution of Congress of the 23d of April, 1782, on an annual pension for life: Their peculiar sufferings, their singular merits and claims to that provision, need only to be known, to interest the feelings of humanity in their behalf: Nothing but a punctual payment of their annual allowance can rescue them from the most complicated misery; and nothing could be a more melancholy and distressing sight, than to behold those who have shed their blood, or lost their limbs, in the service of their country, without a shelter, without a friend, and without the means of obtaining any of the comforts or necessaries of life, compelled to beg their daily bread from door to door. Suffer me to recommend those of this description, belonging to your State, to the warmest patronage of your Excellency and your Legislature.

It is necessary to say but a few words on the third topic which was proposed, and which regards particularly the defence of the republic. As there can be little doubt but Congress will recommend a proper peace-establishment for the United States, in which a due attention will be paid to the importance of placing the militia of the union upon a regular and respectable footing; if this should be the case, I would beg leave to urge the great advantage of it in the strongest terms.

The militia of this country must be considered as the palladium of our security, and the first effectual resort in case of hostility: It is essential, therefore, that the same system should pervade the whole; that the formation and discipline of the militia of the continent, should be absolutely uniform; and that the same species of arms, accoutrements, and military apparatus, should be introduced in every part of the United States: No one, who has not learned it from experience, can conceive the difficulty, expence and confusion, which result from a contrary system, or the vague arrangements which have hitherto prevailed.

If, in treating of political points, a greater latitude than usual has been taken in the course of this address, the importance of the crisis, and the magnitude of the objects in discussion, must be my apology: It is, however, neither my wish nor expectation, that the preceding observations should claim any regard, except so far as they shall appear to be dictated by a good intention; consonant to the immutable rules of justice; calculated to produce a liberal system of policy, and founded on whatever experience may have been acquired by a long and close attention to public business. Here I might speak with the more confidence, from my actual observations; and if it would not swell this letter (already too prolix) beyond the bounds I had prescribed myself, I could demonstrate to every mind, open to conviction, that in less time, and with much less expence than has been incurred, the war might have been brought to the same happy conclusion, if the resources of the continent could have been properly called forth: That the distresses and disappointments which have very often occurred, have, in too many instances, resulted more from a want of energy in the continental government, than a deficiency of means in the particular States: That the inefficacy of measures, arising from the want of an adequate authority in the supreme power, from a partial compliance with the requisitions of Congress in some of the States, and from a failure of punctuality in others, while they tended to damp the zeal of those which were more willing to exert themselves, served also to accumulate the expences of the war, and to frustrate the best concerted plans; and that the discouragement occasioned by the complicated difficulties and embarrassments, in which our affairs were by this means involved, would have long ago produced the dissolution of any army, less patient, less virtuous, and less persevering, than that which I have had the honor to command.—But while I mention those things, which are notorious facts, as the defects of our federal constitution, particularly in the prosecution of a war, I beg it may be understood, that as I have ever taken a pleasure in gratefully acknowledging the assistance and support I have derived from every class of citizens; so shall I always be happy to do justice to the unparalleled exertions of the individual States, on many interesting occasions.

I have thus freely disclosed what I wished to make known before I surrendered up my public trust to those who committed it to me: The task is now accomplished; I now bid adieu to your Excellency, as the Chief Magistrate of your State; at the same time I bid a last farewell to the cares of office, and all the employments of public life.

It remains, then, to be my final and only request, that your Excellency will communicate these sentiments to your Legislature, at their next meeting; and that they may be considered as the legacy of one who has ardently wished, on all occasions, to be useful to his country, and who, even in the shade of retirement, will not fail to implore the divine benediction upon it.

I now make it my earnest prayer, that God would have you, and the State over which you preside, in his holy protection; that he would incline the hearts of the citizens to cultivate a spirit of subordination and obedience to government; to entertain a brotherly affection and love for one another, for their fellow-citizens of the United States at large, and particularly for their brethren who have served in the field; and finally, that he would most graciously be pleased to dispose us all to do justice, to love mercy, and to demean ourselves with that charity, humility and pacific temper of mind, which were the characteristics of the Divine Author of our blessed religion; without an humble imitation of whose example, in these things, we can never hope to be a happy nation.

# Destined for the History Books

☙ ❧

WILLIAM GORDON TO GEORGE WASHINGTON,
JAMAICA PLAIN, 19 JUNE 1783

Though I have not had the pleasure of an answer, owing to the multiplicity of your engagements, yet by a few lines, from New York I have learnt that You was so obliging as to comply with my request.

We have now attained to a certainty of peace, upon which You have my most hearty congratulations. Your name will be deservedly written with honor & respect in every history of America. May it be written & perpetuated in the Lamb's book of life & a better salvation, at a distant glorious exit from off this stage of mortality, be bestowed upon You, that your Excellency has been instrumental of procuring for the United States!

The swordsman will pay little attention to any more than your military feats; but the gownsman will admire You for your sacred regards to the civil authority & the rights of citizens wherever You have been. I rejoice much at the thought that the war is closed, without my ever hearing or knowing, that You have in any one instance set at defiance or encroached upon the civil power; or that under all your sufferings & provocations through the failure of the states to support You, You have used the sword to supply your necessities. The counter-manoeuvre whereby You disappointed the designs of heated spirits in the army has added new lustre to Your character; & the glory of your military course will be completed, when the gentlemen of the army have peaceably quitted the camp & assumed their former relation of good citizens in their respective states.

We are deeply indebted to Messrs. Adams, Jay & Laurens for having negotiated so good a peace: & Dr. Franklin was of great service by his sagacity & influence. Cannot suppose You are a stranger to particulars, & therefore do not mention them. Such were the judicious manoeuvres of Mr. Adams, that the French nobility could not compliment him high enough without involving therein a compliment to your Excellency— "You are the Washington in politics." The papers mention a design on the part of France to confer honors upon You. They have none to bestow equal to what You have already received, & American[s] I trust will not be shaded by placing Europe as above them....

—Washington Papers, Library of Congress. The Reverend William Gordon had emigrated to America in 1770, and two years later was ordained pastor of the Third Congregational Church in Roxbury, Mass. In 1776 he decided to write a history of the American Revolution, which was published in three volumes in 1788.

# We Need to be "Better Cemented"

⚤ ⚤

GEORGE WASHINGTON TO WILLIAM GORDON,
HEADQUARTERS, NEWBURGH, N.Y., 8 JULY 1783

Your favor of the 19th. of June came to my hands on Sunday last by the Southern Mail—from this circumstance, & the date of it I conclude it has been to Philadelphia—a mistake not very unusual for the Postmaster at Fishkiln to commit.—

I delayed not a moment to forwd. the letters which came to me under your cover of the 26th. of Feby. to New York—I did not answer the letter which accompanied them in due Season—not so much from the hurry of business, as because my Sentiments on the essential part of it had been communicated to you before—and because the Annunciation of Peace, which came close upon the heels of it, put an end to all speculative opinions with respect to the time & terms of it.

I now thank you for your kind congratulations on this event—I feel sensibly the flattering expressions, & fervent wishes with which you have accompanied them—and make a tender of mine, with much cordiality, in return.—It now rests with the Confederated Powers, by the line of conduct they mean to adopt, to make this Country great, happy, & respectable; or to sink it into littleness—worse perhaps—into Anarchy & Confusion; for certain I am, that unless adequate Powers are given to Congress for the *general* purposes of the Federal Union that we shall soon moulder into dust and become contemptable in the Eyes of Europe, if we are not made the sport of their Politicks—to suppose that the general concern of this Country can be directed by thirteen heads, or one head without competent powers, is a solecism, the bad effects of which every Man who had had the practical knowledge to judge from, that I have, is fully convinced of; tho' none perhaps has felt them in so forcible, & distressing a degree.— The People at large, and at a distance from the theatre of Action, who only know that the Machine was kept in motion, and that they are at last arrived at the first object of their Wishes are satisfied with the event, without investigating the causes of the slow progress to it, or of the Expences which have accrued & which they now seem unwilling to pay—great part of which has arisen from that want of energy in the Federal Constitution which I am complaining of, and which I wish to see given to it by a Convention of the People, instead of hearing it remarked that as we have worked through an arduous contest with the Powers Congress already have (but which, by the by, have been gradually diminishing) why should they be invested with more?—

To say nothing of the invisible workings of Providence, which has conducted us through difficulties where no human foresight could point the way; it will appear evident to a close Examiner, that there has been a concatenation of causes to produce this Event; which in all probability at no time, or under any other Circumstances, will combine again—We deceive ourselves therefore by this mode of reasoning, and what would be much worse, we may bring ruin upon ourselves by attempting to carry it into practice.

We are known by no other character among Nations than as the United States—Massachusetts or Virginia is no better defined, nor any more thought of by Foreign Powers than the County of Worcester in Massachusetts is by Virginia, or Gloucester County in Virginia is by Massachusetts (respectable as they are); and yet these Counties, with as much propriety might oppose themselves to the Laws of the State in wch. they are, as an Individual State can oppose itself to the Federal Government, by which it is, or ought to be bound.— Each of these Counties has, no doubt, its local polity & Interests.—These should be attended to, & brought before their respective legislatures with all the force their importance merits; but when they come in contact with the general Interest of the State—when superior considerations preponderate in favor of the whole— their Voices should be heard no more—so should it be with individual States when compared to the Union— Otherwise I think it may properly be asked for what purpose do we farcically pretend to be United?—Why do Congress spend Months together in deliberating upon, debating, & digesting plans, which are made as palatable, & as wholesome to the Constitution of this Country as the nature of things will admit of, when some States will pay no attention to them, & others regard them but partially; by which means all those evils which proceed from delay, are felt by the whole; while the compliant States are not only suffering by these neglects, but in many instances are injured most capitally by their own exertions; which are wasted for want of the United effort.—A hundd. thousand men coming one after another cannot move a Ton weight—but the united strength of 50 would transport it with ease.—so has it been with [a] great part of the expence which has been incurred [during] this War. In a Word, I think the blood & treasure which has been spent in it has been lavished to little purpose, unless we can be better Cemented; and that is not to be effected while so little attention is paid to the recommendations of the Sovereign Power.

To me it would seem not more absurd, to hear a traveller, who was setting out on a long journey, declare he would take no Money in his pocket to defray the Expences of it but rather depend upon chance & charity lest he should misapply it, than are the expressions of so much fear of the powers and means of Congress. For Heavens sake who are Congress?—are they not Creatures of the People, amenable to them for their Conduct, and dependant from day to day on their breath?—Where then can be the danger of giving them such Powers as are adequate to the great ends of Government, and to all the general purposes of the Confederation (I repeat the word *genl*, because I am no advocate for their having to do with the particular policy of any State, further than it concerns the Union at large).—What may be the consequences if they have not these Powers I am at no loss to guess; and deprecate the worst; for sure I am, we shall, in a little time, become as contemptable in the great Scale of Politicks as we now have it in our power to be respectable—and that, when the band of Union gets once broken, every thing ruinous to our future prospects is to be apprehended—the best that can come of it, in my humble opinion is, that we shall sink into obscurity, unless our Civil broils should keep us in remembrance & fill the page of history with the direful consequences of them.—

You say that, Congress loose time by pressing a mode that does not accord with the genius of the People, & will thereby, endanger the Union—and that it is the quantum they want—Permit me to ask if the quantum has not already been demanded?—Whether it has been obtained?—and whence proceed the accumulated evils & poignant distresses of many of the public Creditors,—particularly in the Army?—For my own part I hesitate not a moment to confess, that I see nothing wherein the Union is endangered by the late Requisition of that body, but a prospect of much good, justice, & propriety from the compliance with it.—I know of no Tax more convenient—none so agreeable, as that which every Man may pay, or let it alone as his con-

venience, abilities, or Inclination shall prompt.—I am
therefore a warm friend to the Impost.[1] . . .

—Washington Papers, Library of Congress

[1] In April 1783 Congress proposed that the states give it the
power to levy import duties for 25 years.

# Recorded in the
# Brightest Pages of History

🌿 🌿

## SAMUEL ADAMS AND TRISTRAM DALTON
## TO GEORGE WASHINGTON, BOSTON, 10 JULY 1783

The Senate and House of Representatives of the
Commonwealth of Massachusetts in General Court Assembled, take this Opportunity of congratulating you,
on the happy Return of Peace.—

Your Excellency, we are assured, will join with us,
in the Warmest Expressions of Gratitude to the Supreme Ruler of the Universe, under whose Influence
and Direction the Struggles of a virtuous & free People
have terminated in a Revolution which excites the Admiration of the World.—

Guided by *his* all-wise Providence, your Country
early fixed her Eyes upon you: And confiding in those
eminent Qualities which you possess, appointed you
to the Command of her Armies.—

The Wisdom of your Conduct in the Discharge of
that important Trust, has given a compleat sanction to
the Appointment, and crown'd the most heighten'd
Expectations.—

In every Stage of the arduous Conflict, what trying Scenes have you not passed through! What Hardships have you not endured! What Dangers have you not encountered!—May Heaven reward your unremmitted Exertions!—May you long live, beloved by a grateful Country, & partaking largely in the Enjoyment of these inestimable Blessings, which you have been so eminently instrumental in securing for us.—

While Patriots shall not cease to applaud that sacred Attachment which you have constantly manifested to *the Rights of Citizens*—too often violated by Men in Arms—

Your *Military* Virtues & Atchievements will be deeply recorded in the Breasts of your Countrymen & their Posterity, and make the brightest Pages in the History of Mankind—

—Washington Papers, Library of Congress. Adams was president of the Massachusetts Senate and Dalton was speaker of the state House of Representatives.

# "Revered at Home and Abroad"

卐 卐

SOUTH CAROLINA GOVERNOR BENJAMIN GUERARD
TO GEORGE WASHINGTON, CHARLESTOWN,
1 AUGUST 1783

I have had the honor of receiving your letter of the 14th of June which with cheerfulness and pleasure I will lay before our Legislature at their next sitting—I thank you, Sir, for your Congratulations on the happy and glorious event of the peace, an event the most heartfelt and joyful, as our Country is not only thereby relieved from the accumulated and almost insuperable distresses it was plunged into by the unnatural and cruel war, but *through you* by the permission of the Director of all human Events it had obtained and enjoys "among the powers of the Earth, the separate and equal station to which the laws of nature and of nature's God entitle us"[1]—In return I request most heartily to Congratulate your Excellency, that you have lived to see the accomplishment of the great object of your important appointment charge and trust—that you have acquired for your Country, by your Patriotism, Integrity Benevolence, Wisdom, Honour and Valour—Peace, Freedom, Happiness, Sovereignty and Independence—And that you have Survived the hardships, painful anxieties, and great Fatigues and escaped the numerous perils you were unavoidably exposed to during the various and long doubtful conflict—May a character So great and finished, revered at home and abroad long enjoy that retreat he left reluctantly and return to it with joy in undisturbed health, repose, comfort, and happiness— and—May you, Sir long live for the good of your Country and Countrymen to stimulate them by your examples to wise, great, magnificent, disinterested, honourable, just, impartial pure and right thoughts and actions.—

—Washington Papers, Library of Congress.

[1]Quoted from the Declaration of Independence.

# "Little Less Than Adored"

※ ※

NATHANAEL GREENE TO GEORGE WASHINGTON,
CHARLESTOWN, 8 AUGUST 1783

... The Assembly of this State have rejected the impost Act recommended by Congress. Had your circular letter been printed a fortnight earlier, I am persuaded it would have brought them in to the measure. On once reading in the house it produced an alteration of sentiment of more than one-quarter of the Members. The force and affection with which it was written made everyone seem to embrace it with Avidity. You were admired before; you are little less than adored now. The recommendation of Congress had but a feeble influence until it was supported by yours. Altho the State did not come into the plan recommended by Congress, they have laid a tax of five percent on the Authority of the State: to be solely for the Continental use. This I attribute entirely to your letter. Its effects have been astonishing. . . .

—Washington Papers, Library of Congress. Greene was commander of the Southern Department of the Continental Army.

# The Solemn Resignation

≛ ≛

James Tilton to Gunning Bedford,
Annapolis, 25 December 1783

The General came to town last friday, and announced his arrival, by a letter to congress, requesting to know, in what manner they chused he should resign his authority; whether by private letter or public audience? The latter was preferred without hesitation. Some etiquette being settled on saturday, a public dinner was ordered on monday and the audience to be on tuesday. The feast on monday was the most extraordinary I ever attended. Between 2 and 3 hundred Gentn: dined together in the *ball-room*. The number of cheerful voices, with the clangor of knives and forks made a din of a very extraordinary nature and most delightful influence. Every man seemed to be in heaven or so absored in the pleasures of imagination, as to neglect the more sordid appetites, for not a soul got drunk, though there was wine in plenty and the usual number of 13 toasts drank, besides one given afterwards by the General which you ought to be acquainted with: it is as follows. "Competent powers to congress for general purposes."

In the evening of the same day, the Governor gave a ball at the State House. To light the rooms every window was illuminated. Here the company was equally numerous, and more brilliant, consisting of ladies and Gentn: Such was my villanous awkwardness, that I could not venture to dance on this occasion, you must therefore annex to it a cleverer Idea, than is to be expected from such a mortified whelp as I am. The General danced every set, that all the ladies might have the pleasure of dancing with him, or as it has since been handsomely expressed, *get a touch of him.*

Tuesday morning, Congress met, and took their seats in order, all covered.[1] At twelve o'clock the General was introduced by the Secretary, and seated opposite to the president [Thomas Mifflin], until the throng, that filled all the avenues, were so disposed of so as to behold the solemnity. The ladies occupied the gallery as full as it would hold, the Gentn: crouded below stairs. Silence ordered, by the Secretary, the Genl. rose and bowed to congress, who uncovered, but did not bow. He then delivered his speech, and at the close of it drew his commission from his bosem and handed it to the president. The president replied in a set speech, the General bowed again to Congress, they uncovered and the General retired. After a little pause until the company withdrew, Congress adjourned. The General then steped into the room again, bid every member farewell and rode off from the door, intent upon eating his christmas dinner at home. Many of the spectators, particularly the fair ones shed tears, on this solemn and affecting occasion.

—John C. Fitzpatrick ed., *The Writings of George Washington from the Original Manuscript Sources, 1745–1799* (39 vols., Washington, D.C., 1931–1944), XXVII, 285n–86n. Tilton and Bedford represented Delaware in Congress.

[1] A reference to the delegates wearing their hats.

# "A Spectacle
Inexpressibly Solemn
and Affecting"

粟 粟

JAMES MCHENRY TO MARGARET CALDWELL,
ANNAPOLIS, 23 DECEMBER 1783

... To day my love the General at a public audience
made a deposit of his commission and in a very pathetic
manner took leave of Congress. It was a solemn and
affecting spectacle; such an one as history does not
present. The spectators all wept, and there was hardly
a member of Congress who did not drop tears. The
General's hand which held the address shook as he read
it. When he spoke of the officers who had composed
his family, and recommended those who had continued
in it to the present moment to the favorable notice of
Congress he was obliged to support the paper with
both hands. But when he commended the interests of
his dearest country to almighty God, and those who
had the superintendence of them to his holy keeping,
his voice faultered and sunk, and the whole house felt
his agitations. After the pause which was necessary for
him to recover himself, he proceeded to say in the most
penetrating manner, "Having now finished the work
assigned me I retire from the great theatre of action,
and bidding an affectionate farewell to this august body
under whose orders I have so long acted I here offer
my commission and take leave of all the employments
of public life." So saying he drew out from his bosom
his commission and delivered it up to the president of
Congress. He then returned to his station, when the
president read the reply that had been prepared—but I

thought without any shew of feeling, tho' with much dignity.

This is only a sketch of the scene. But, were I to write you a long letter I could not convey to you the whole. So many circumstances crowded into view and gave rise to so many affecting emotions. The events of the revolution just accomplished—the new situation into which it had thrown the affairs of the world—the great man who had borne so conspicuous a figure in it, in the act of relinquishing all public employments to return to private life—the past—the present—the future—the manner—the occasion—all conspired to render it a spectacle inexpressibly solemn and affecting. . . .

—Edmund C. Burnett, ed., *Letters of Members of the Continental Congress* (8 vols., Washington, D.C., 1921–1936), VII, 394–95. McHenry was a Maryland delegate to Congress. Two weeks later, he and Margaret Caldwell were married.

# "*Cincinnatus*"

This poem was written by Philip Freneau in December 1783. It became one of the "readings" in Noah Webster's *An American Selection of Lessons in Reading and Speaking* . . . (3rd ed., Philadelphia, 1787), 368–71. The *Massachusetts Centinel*, 1 August 1789, reprinted a lengthy excerpt.

꽃 꽃

*Verses occasioned by General* Washington's *arrival in Philadelphia, on his way to his seat in Virginia.*

The great, unequal conflict past,
The Briton banish'd from our shore,
Peace, heav'n-descended, comes at last,
And hostile nations rage no more;
 From fields of death the weary swain
 Returning, seeks his native plain.
In every vale she smiles serene,
Freedom's bright stars more radiant rise,
New charms she adds to every scene,
Her brighter sun illumes our skies;
 Remotest realms admiring stand,
 And hail the hero of our land;
He comes!—the Genius of these lands—
Fame's thousand tongues his worth confess,
Who conquer'd with his suffering bands
And grew immortal by distress:
 Thus calms succeed the stormy blast,
 And valor is repaid at last.
O Washington!—thrice glorious name,
What due rewards can man decree—
Empires are far below thy aim,
And sceptres have no charms for thee;
 Virtue alone has thy regard,

30

And she must be thy great reward.
Encircled by extorted power,
Monarchs must envy thy retreat,
Who cast, in some ill fated hour,
Their country's freedom at their feet;
    'Twas thine to act a nobler part
    For injur'd Freedom had thy heart.
For ravag'd realms and conquer'd seas
Rome gave the great imperial prize,
And, swell'd with pride, for seats like these,
Transferr'd her heroes to the skies:—
    A brighter scene your deeds display,
    You gain those hearts a different way.
When Faction rear'd her shaky head,
And join'd with tyrants to destroy,
Where'er you march'd the monster fled,
Tim'rous her arrows to employ;
    Hosts catch'd from you a bolder flame,
    And despots trembled at your name.
Ere war's dread horrors ceas'd to reign
What leader could your place supply?—
Chiefs crouded to the embattled plain,
Prepar'd to conquer or to die—
    Heroes arose—but none like you
    Could save our lives and freedom too.
In swelling verse let kings be read,
And princes shine in polish'd prose;
Without such aid your triumphs spread
Where'er the convex ocean flows,
    To Indian worlds by seas embrac'd,
    And Tartar, tyrant of the waste.
Throughout the east you gain applause,
And soon the old world, taught by you,
Shall blush to own her barbarous laws,
Shall learn instruction from the new:
    Monarchs shall hear the humble plea,
    Nor urge too far the proud decree.
Despising pomp and vain parade,

At home you stay, while France and Spain
The secret, ardent wish convey'd,
And hail'd you to their shores in vain:
    In Vernon's groves you shun the throne,
    Admir'd by kings, but seen by none.
Your fame, thus spread to distant lands,
May envy's fiercest blasts endure,
Like Egypt's pyramids it stands,
Built on a basis more secure;
    Time's latest age shall own in you
    The patriot and the statesman too.
Nor hurrying from the busy scene,
Where thy Potowmack's waters flow,
May'st thou enjoy thy rural reign,
And every earthly blessing know;
    Thus *He** who Rome's proud legions sway'd,
    Return'd, and sought his sylvan shade.
Not less in wisdom than in war
Freedom shall still employ your mind,
Slavery shall vanish, wide and far,
'Till not a trace is left behind;
    Your counsels not bestow'd in vain
    Shall still protect this infant reign.
So when the bright, all-cheering sun
From our contracted view retires,
Though fools may think his race is run,
On other worlds he lights his fires:
    Cold climes beneath his influence glow,
    And frozen rivers learn to flow.
O say, thou great, exalted name!
What muse can boast of equal lays,
Thy worth disdains all vulgar fame,
Transcends the noblest poet's praise.
    Art soars unequal to the flight,
    And genius sickens at the height.
For states redeem'd—our western reign

*Cincinnatus.

Restor'd by thee to milder sway,
Thy conscious glory shall remain
When this great globe is swept away,
   And all is lost that pride admires,
   And all the pageant scene expires.

—Noah Webster, *An American Selection of Lessons in Reading and Speaking* . . . (3rd ed., Philadelphia, 1787), 368–71.

# The General's *"Political Creed"*

娑 婆

## GEORGE WASHINGTON TO BENJAMIN HARRISON, MOUNT VERNON, 18 JANUARY 1784

I have just had the pleasure to receive your letter of the 8th.—for the friendly & affectionate terms in which you have welcomed my return to this Country & to private life; & for the favourable light in which you are pleased to consider, & express your sense of my past services, you have my warmest & most grateful acknowledgments.

That the prospect before us is, as you justly observe, fair, none can deny; but what use we shall make of it, is exceedingly problematical; not but that I believe, all things will come right at last; but like a young heir, come a little prematurely to a large inheritance, we shall wanton & run riot until we have brought our reputation to the brink of ruin, & then like him shall have to labor with the current of opinion, when *compelled*, perhaps, to do what prudence & common policy pointed out as plain as any problem in Euclid, in the first instance.

The disinclination of the individual States to yield competent powers to Congress for the Fœderal Government, their unreasonable jealousy of that body & of one another—& the disposition which seems to pervade each, of being all-wise & all-powerful within itself, will, if there is not a change in the system, be our downfal as a nation.—This is as clear to me as the A, B, C; & I think we have opposed Great Britain, & have arrived at the present state of peace & independency, to very little purpose, if we cannot conquer our own prejudices. The powers of Europe begin to see this, & our newly acquired friends the British, are already & professedly acting upon this ground; & wisely too, if we are determined to persevere in our folly. They know that individual opposition to their measures is futile, & *boast* that we are not sufficiently united as a Nation to give a general one!—Is not the indignity alone, of this declaration, while we are in the very act of peace-making & conciliation, sufficient to stimulate us to vest more extensive & adequate powers in the sovereign of these United States?—For my own part, altho' I am returned to, & am now mingled with the class of private citizens, & like them must suffer all the evils of a Tyranny, or of too great an extension of fœderal powers; I have no fears arising from this source; in my mind, but I have many, & powerful ones indeed which predict the worst consequences from a half-starved, limping Government, that appears to be always moving upon crutches, & tottering at every step. Men, chosen as the Delegates in Congress are, cannot officially be dangerous—they depend upon the breath—nay, they are so much the creatures of the people, under the present Constitution, that they can have no views (which could possibly be carried into execution) nor any interests, distinct from those of their constituents.—My political creed therefore is, to be wise in the choice of Delegates—support them like Gentlemen while they are our Representatives—give them competent powers for all fœderal purposes—support them in the due exercise thereof, & lastly, to compel them to close attendance in Congress during their delegation. These things under the present mode for, & termination of elections, aided by annual instead of constant Sessions, would, or I am exceedingly mistaken, make us one of the most wealthy, happy, respectable & powerful Nations, that ever inhabited the terrestrial Globe—without them, we shall in my opinion soon be every thing which is the direct reverse of them.

—Letterbook, Washington Papers, Library of Congress. Harrison was governor of Virginia.

# "The Solitary Walk"

### GEORGE WASHINGTON TO MARQUIS DE LAFAYETTE, MOUNT VERNON, 1 FEBRUARY 1784

At length my Dear Marquis I am become a private citizen on the banks of the Potomac, & under the shadow of my own Vine & my own Fig-tree,—free from the bustle of a camp & the busy scenes of public life, I am solacing myself with those tranquil enjoyments, of which the Soldier who is ever in pursuit of fame—the Statesman whose watchful days & sleepless nights are spent in devising schemes to promote the welfare of his own—perhaps the ruin of other countries, as if this Globe was insufficient for us all—& the Courtier who is always watching the countenance of his Prince, in hopes of catching a gracious smile, can have very little conception.—I am not only retired from all public employments, but I am retiring within myself; & shall be able to view the solitary walk, & tread the paths of private life with heartfelt satisfaction—Envious of none, I am determined to be pleased with all; & this my dear friend, being the order for my march, I will move gently down the stream of life, until I sleep with my Fathers. . . .

—Letterbook, Washington Papers, Library of Congress.

# The Retirement

MOUNT VERNON.
*An O D E, inscribed to* GENERAL WASHINGTON.
*Written at Mount Vernon, August* 1786.
By *Colonel* HUMPHREYS.

By broad Potowmack's azure tide,
Where Vernon's Mount, in sylvan pride,
    Displays its beauties far:
Great *Washington* to peaceful shades,
Where no unhallow'd wish invades,
    Retir'd from field of war.
Angels might see, with joy, the sage,
Who taught the battle where to rage,
    Or quench'd its spreading flame—
On works of peace employ that hand,
Which wav'd the blade of high command,
    And hew'd the path to fame.
Let others sing his deeds in arms,
A nation sav'd and conquest's charms,
    Posterity shall hear:

'Twas mine, return'd from Europe's courts,[1]
To share his thoughts, partake his sports,
    And soothe his martial ear.
To thee, my friend, these lays belong:
Thy happy seat inspires my song,
    With gay, perenniel blooms;
With fruitage fair, and cool retreats;
Whose bow'ry wilderness of sweets,
    The ambient air perfumes.
Here spring its earliest buds displays,
Here latest on the leafless sprays,
    The plumy people sing:
The vernal show'r, the ripening year,
Th' autumnal store, the winter drear,
    For thee new pleasures bring.
Here lap'd in Philosophic ease,
Within thy walks, beneath thy trees,
    Amidst thine ample farms:
No vulgar converse heroes hold,
But past or future scenes unfold,
    Or dwell on nature's charms.
What wondrous æra have we seen!
Plac'd on this isthmus half between,
    A rude and polish'd state;
We saw the war tempestuous rise,
In arms a world, in blood the skies,
    In doubt an empire's fate.
The storm is calm'd seren'd the heav'n,
And mildly o'er the climes of ev'n,
    Expands th' imperial day:
"Oh God, the source of light supreme,
"Shed on our dusky morn a gleam,
    "To guide our doubtful way!
"Restrain, dread pow'r, our land from crimes!

[1]From 1784 to 1786 Humphreys served in England and France as secretary to the U.S. Commission for Negotiating Treaties of Commerce with Foreign Powers.

"What seeks, tho' blest beyond all times,
    "So querulous an age?
"What means to freedom such disgust;
"Of change, of annarchy, the lust,
    "The fickleness and rage?"
So spoke his country's friend, with sighs,
To find that country still despise
    The LEGACY he gave—
And half he fear'd his toils were vain,
And much that man would court a chain,
    And live through vice a slave.
A transient gloom o'ercast his mind;
Yet still on providence reclin'd,
    The patriot fond believ'd,
That pow'r benign, too much had done,
To leave an empire's task begun,
    Imperfectly achiev'd.
Thus buoy'd with hope, with virtue blest,
Of ev'ry human bliss possest,
    He meets the happier hours:
His skies assume a lovelier blue,
His prospects brighter rise to view,
    And fairer bloom his flow'rs.

—Philadelphia *Columbian Magazine*, January 1787. David Humphreys of Connecticut had served as aide-de-camp to Washington during the end of the war. He and the General developed a warm personal friendship that lasted throughout Washington's life.

# "A Rare Phænomenon"

## A RARE PHÆNOMENON.

While fraud and av'rice reign in every breast,
And merit sinks, by prosp'rous guilt oppress'd;
While wealth and favor perfidy adorn,
And wretched honesty the ruffian's scorn;
While fierce ambition, like a headlong flood,
Insatiate, deluges the globe with blood:
O barb'rous times! Vice triumphs undisguis'd,
Virtue's abash'd, derided and despis'd!
While a perverted world, by truth unaw'd,
Successful guile and pravity applaud;
Yet in a tainted and discolor'd age,
One rare example shines, one star t'engage
Our wonder, worth transcending far all praise,
'Tis Virtue's self with unextinguish'd rays:
'Tis Washington retir'd to life's still scene,
Whose claim like Cæsar's, legion's cou'd sustain;
Whom boundless trust ne'er tempted to betray,
Nor power impell'd to arbitrary sway.
Such Washington, his rescu'd country's theme,
Columbia's glory, 'minish'd Britain's shame.
Too weak the muse, th' illustrious chief to sing,
A private citizen, who might be king.

                                    CINNA.[1]

—Philadelphia *Columbian Magazine*, November 1787. Reprinted in the Charleston, S.C., *City Gazette*, 14 January
1788.

[1]Roman poet mistakenly killed by the mob at Caesar's funeral.

# *Genius of Freedom*

※ ※

## ACROSTICK.

G reat in the martial field, in council wise;
E ach virtue guides thee in thy pleasing way,
O n wings triumphant, how thy glories rise!
R efulgent as th' unclouded God of day!
G *eorge*[1] on his sea girt throne beholds his *sun*,
E clips'd forever by a WASHINGTON!

W hen war's tumalt'ous bloody front alarm'd;
A nd *civil discord* ev'ry *torch* had fir'd;
S erenely brave, the tyrants thou disarm'd,
H ence, at thy frown, *Britannia's host* retir'd.
I n peace; reverting to thy Vernon's stream;
N o views ambitious, pointed thee to thrones;
G ENIUS of FREEDOM, THOU art hail'd supreme,
T he chosen guardian of Columbia's sons.
O n *brass* and *marble* shall thy *deeds* remain;
N o time's corroding breath can blight thy fame.

—*Massachusetts Magazine*, September 1789

[1]George III.

# A Day of Ecstacy

&#x8CA2; &#x8CA2;

## ODE
ON THE BIRTHDAY OF THE PRESIDENT
OF THE UNITED STATES.

Let every muse attune the lay,
And hail with extasy THIS DAY
   Which gave our Hero birth:
Let every Freeman shout and sing,
Their gratulations joyful bring,
And cause the Arch above to ring
   With endless mirth.

With drums and trumpets rend the air;
On Fame's triumphant wing declare,
   His matchless deeds:
Whose name eternally shall rise,
And listening worlds his merit prize;
His glory shines beyond the skies,
   From Heaven proceeds.

Columbia's first and favourite Son,
Has ancient Heroes all outdone;
   His country sav'd
Proud Briton's sons did he subdue;
Like CINCINNATUS then withdrew,
Content like him to take the plough,
   In VERNON's shade.

The Hero, Patriot, Warrior, Sage,
Shall be extroll'd thro' every age,
   While Planets roll:
The distant nations shall admire,
And catch the spark from Freedom's fire,

41

That sacred altar shall inspire;
　　From Pole to Pole.

And when kind Heaven shall judge it fit,
That he his grateful Land should quit,
　　To Realms above;
May freedom's Marty'rs watch his clay,
While Guardian Angel's shall convey,
His soul to climes of Endless Day,
　　To sing redeeming Love.

Boston, February 11, 1790.

—Boston *Independent Chronicle*, 11 February 1790. Reprinted in the *Massachusetts Centinel*, 13 February 1790.

# The Immortal Washington

ODE,

*Sung by a number of the Citizens of* ROXBURY, *on the Evening of the Birth-day of our beloved* PRESIDENT.

Join! join th' exalted lay!
Come! hail th' auspicious day
　　That gave *Him* birth:
Who led Columbia's arms
Through horrid war's alarms;
Now, bright in glory's charms,
　　Shines round the earth!

Sound! sound the Hero's fame!
Immortalize his name

In deathless song!
See, shining pow'rs display'd!
There *Mars* his *Ægis* spread,[1]
And here the *martial Maid*[2]
Aids him along!

See! see the Chief disclaim
Th' immortal wreath of Fame
      The world bestow'd;
His country's liberty,
The palm of victory,
In humble piety
      Ascrib'd to GOD.

See! see the Chief disarm,
And to his native farm
      Retire, renown'd.
Like CINCINNATUS now
He holds the humble plough,
While round the Hero's brow
      The laurel's bound.

The happy arts of Peace
In harmony possess
      His noble mind;
Within his glowing breast
Will real worth depress'd,
And innocence distress'd,
      Compassion find.

The philanthropick mind,
The good of all mankind,
      Whose wishes bound;

[1]A reference to the battle shield of Mars, the god of war.
[2]A reference to Minerva, who sprang forth from Jupiter's brain fully grown and armed. She was a fierce battle-goddess when defending the state.

And warmer patriot zeal,
To aid the common weal;
And arts and science still
     Dispensing round.

No titles charm his ear;
Them, and the flatterer,
     At once declines;
Contemning stars and strings
(The dirty gifts of Kings)—
His name, such paltry things,
     Alone outshines.

Wake! wake each voice and string!
Let length'ning pæans ring
     'Till air be torn!
Join! join each voice as one—
For, lo! Columbia's son,
Th' immortal WASHINGTON,
     To-day was born!

—*Massachusetts Centinel*, 17 February 1790.

# II

RETIREMENT
ABANDONED

*The Constitutional Convention*

I N 1787 GEORGE WASHINGTON was the most popular
man in America. When he abandoned power in
1783, Americans were convinced that he was truly
unique—a man uncorrupted by power. Thus, when a
convention was called to revise the Articles of Confederation, the Virginia legislature quite logically elected
Washington to lead the state's delegation. With Washington appointed, Virginia's seriousness would be apparent, and the other states would appoint prominent
delegates. Furthermore, Americans would have confidence in the convention knowing that the former commander in chief would thwart any attempts to create a
monarchical or aristocratical government.

Throughout November and December 1786, James
Madison tried to convince Washington of the importance of the Constitutional Convention and his attendance. On 6 December 1786 Governor Edmund
Randolph notified Washington officially of his appointment and pleaded with the General to accept the position. There was still, Randolph said, "one ray of hope
that those who began, carried on, and consummated
the Revolution, can yet rescue America from the impending ruin." Washington, however, declined the
appointment.

Washington gave several reasons for his refusal to attend the Constitutional Convention scheduled to meet in Philadelphia in May. He had promised in his June 1783 letter to the state executives that he would never again return to public life. He did not want to break that promise. Washington also worried about the legality of the Convention, which was initially called by the delegates to the Annapolis Convention. Once Congress sanctioned the proposed Constitution on 21 February 1787, this concern abated. But Washington also had personal reasons for not attending the Convention. He was bothered with rheumatism, and, late in April 1787, he received word that his mother and sister were near death. Washington had also already informed the Society of the Cincinnati that he would be unable to attend its general triennial convention, which was to be held simultaneously in Philadelphia in May. As president general of the society, Washington was expected to attend the convention of former army officers. But, somewhat embarrassed by the attacks on the society as a hereditary, aristocratic organization, Washington had hoped not to be reelected its president—an impossibility if he attended the convention. Thus, if Washington now accepted an appointment to the Constitutional Convention, he worried that he would appear duplicitous in the eyes of his former comrades.

In February and March 1787 Washington sought advice from David Humphreys of Connecticut and Henry Knox of Massachusetts. The former had been one of the General's aides during the war; the latter had commanded the country's artillery. In 1787 Knox was stationed in New York City as the Confederation's Secretary at War. Both men saw the dangers in Washington attending the Convention; Knox, however, saw some benefits. Thus, Humphreys recommended against attending, while Knox encouraged the General to attend.

After much soul searching, Washington realized that his refusal to attend the Convention might be interpreted as an act against republicanism. Why would Washington refuse an appointment to the Convention which offered perhaps the last chance America had to peacefully revise the Articles of Confederation? Did Washington have ulterior motives? Did he wish for failure in Philadelphia so that the people would demand that he accept power and restore stability, prosperity and honor to the country he had so recently freed from the tyranny of an imperial power in London? After four months of agonizing, Washington finally consented to leave Mount Vernon on public business.

# A Favorable Dawn
## Turns Cloudy

⚓ ⚓

GEORGE WASHINGTON TO JAMES MADISON,
MOUNT VERNON, 5 NOVEMBER 1786

I thank you for the communications in your letter
of the first inst. The decision of the House on the
question respecting a paper emission, is portentous I
hope, of an auspicious Session. It may certainly be
classed among the important questions of the present
day; and merited the serious consideration of the Assembly. Fain would I hope, that the great, & most important of all objects—the fœderal governmt.—may be
considered with that calm & deliberate attention which
the magnitude of it so loudly calls for at this critical
moment. Let prejudices, unreasonable jealousies, and
local interest yield to reason and liberality. Let us look
to our National character, and to things beyond the
present period. No morn ever dawned more favourable
than ours did—and no day was ever more clouded than
the present! Wisdom, & good examples are necessary
at this time to rescue the political machine from the
impending storm. Virginia has now an opportunity to
set the latter, and has enough of the former, I hope, to
take the lead in promoting this great & arduous work.
Without some alteration in our political creed, the su-
perstructure we have been seven years raising at the
expence of much blood and treasure, must fall. We are
fast verging to anarchy & confusion! A letter which I
have just received from Genl Knox, who had just returned from Massachusetts (whither he had been sent
by Congress consequent of the commotion in that State)
is replete with melancholy information of the temper

48

& designs of a considerable part of that people.[1] Among other things he says, "there creed is, that the property of the United States, has been protected from confiscation of Britain by the joint exertions of *all*, and therefore ought to be the *common property* of all. And he that attempts opposition to this creed is an enemy to equity & justice, & ought to be swept from off the face of the Earth." Again "They are determined to anihilate all debts public & private, and have Agrarian Laws, which are easily effected by the means of unfunded paper Money which shall be a tender in all cases whatever." He adds, "The numbers of these people amount in Massachusetts to about one fifth part of several populous Counties, and to these may be collected, people of similar sentiments from the States of Rhode Island, Connecticut, & New Hampshire so as to constitute a body of twelve or fifteen thousand desperate, and unprincipled men. They are chiefly of the young & active part of the Community."

How melancholy is the reflection, that in so short a space, we should have made such large strides towards fulfilling the prediction of our transatlantic foe! "Leave them to themselves, and their government will soon dissolve." Will not the wise & good strive hard to avert this evil? Or will their supineness suffer ignorance and the arts of self interested designing disaffected & desperate characters, to involve this rising empire in wretchedness & contempt? What stronger evidence can be given of the want of energy in our governments than these disorders? If there exists not a power to check them, what security has a man of life, liberty, or property? To you, I am sure I need not add aught on this subject, the consequences of a lax, or inefficient government, are too obvious to be dwelt on. Thirteen sovereignties pulling against each other, and all tugging at the fœderal head will soon bring ruin on the whole;

[1]Shays's Rebellion.

49

whereas a liberal, and energetic Constitution, well guarded, & closely watched, to prevent incroachments, might restore us to that degree of respectability & consequence, to which we had a fair claim, & the brightest prospect of attaining.

—Madison Papers, Library of Congress.

# "Leaning to the Side of Hope"

寒寒

## JAMES MADISON TO GEORGE WASHINGTON, RICHMOND, 8 NOVEMBER 1786

I am just honoured with your favor of the 5th. inst. The intelligence from Genl. Knox is gloomy indeed, but is less so than the colours in which I had it thro' another channel. If the lessons which it inculcates should not work the proper impressions on the American Public, it will be proof that our case is desperate. Judging from the present temper and apparent views of our Assembly, I have some ground for leaning to the side of Hope. The vote against Paper money has been followed by two others of great importance. By one of them sundry petitions for applying a scale of depreciation to the Military Certificates was *unanimously* rejected. By the other the expediency of complying with the Recomm[end]ation from Annapolis in favor of a general revision of the federal System was *unanimously* agreed to. A bill for the purpose is now depending and in a form which attests the most federal spirit. As no opposition has been yet made and it is ready for the third reading, I expect it will soon be before the public.[1] It has been thought advisable to give this subject a very solemn dress, and all the weight which could be derived from a single State. This idea will also be pursued in the selection of characters to represent Virga. in the federal Convention. You will infer our earnestness on this point from the liberty which will be used of placing your name at the head of them. How far this liberty may correspond with the ideas by which you ought to be governed will be best decided where it must ultimately be decided. In every event it will assist powerfully in marking the zeal of our Legislature, and its opinion of the magnitude of the occasion. . . .

—Washington Papers, Library of Congress.

[1]On 9 November 1786 the Virginia House of Delegates approved a bill authorizing the appointment of delegates to the Constitutional Convention. The Senate concurred on 23 November, and on 4 December the legislature elected seven delegates, including Washington and Madison.

# *"Threatening Clouds"*

෴

## George Washington to James Madison, Mount Vernon, 18 November 1786

Not having sent to the Post Office with my usual regularity, your favor of the 8th. did not reach me in time for an earlier acknowledgment than of this date.

It gives me the most sensible pleasure to hear that the Acts of the present Session, are marked with wisdom, justice & liberality. They are the palladium of good policy, & the only paths that lead to national happiness. Would to God every State would let these be the leading features of their constituents characters: those threatening clouds which seem ready to burst on the Confederacy, would soon dispel. The unanimity with which the Bill was received, for appointing commissioners agreeably to the recommendation of the Convention at Annapolis; and the uninterrupted progress it has met with since, are indications of a favourable issue. It is a measure of equal necessity & magnitude; & may be the spring of reanimation.

Altho' I have bid a public adieu to the public walks of life, & had resolved never more to tread that theatre; yet, if upon an occasion so interesting to the well-being of the confederacy it should have been the wish of the assembly that I should have been an associate in the business of revising the fœderal System; I should, from a sense of the obligation I am under for repeated proofs of confidence in me, more than from any opinion I should have entertained of my usefulness, have obeyed its call; but it is now out of my power to do this with any degree of consistency—the cause I will mention.

I presume you heard Sir, that I was first appointed, & have since been rechosen President of the Society of the Cincinnati; & you may have understood also that the triennial Genl. Meeting of this body is to be held in Philada. the first monday in May next. Some particular reasons combining with the peculiar situation of my private concerns; the necessity of paying attention to them; a wish for retirement & relaxation from public cares, and rheumatic pains which I begin to feel very sensibly, induced me on the 31st. ulto. to address a circular letter to each State society informing them of my intention not to be at the next Meeting, & of my desire not to be re-chosen President. The Vice President [Horatio Gates] is also informed of this, that the business of the Society may not be impeded by my absence. Under these circumstances it will readily be perceived that I could not appear at the same time & place on any other occasion, without giving offence to a very respectable & deserving part of the community—the late officers of the American Army. . . .

—Madison Papers, Library of Congress.

# "One Ray of Hope"

※ ※

## GOV. EDMUND RANDOLPH TO GEORGE WASHINGTON, RICHMOND, 6 DECEMBER 1786

By the enclosed Act you will readily discover, that the Assembly are alarmed at the Storms, which threaten the United States. What our enemies have foretold, seems to be hastening to its accomplishment; and cannot be frustrated but by an instantaneous zealous & steady Union among the friends of the fœderal Government: To you I need not press our present dangers. The inefficiency of Congress you have often felt in your Official Character: the increasing languor of our associated republics you hourly see: and a dissolution would be I know to you a source of the deepest mortification.

I freely then intreat you to accept the Unanimous appointment of the General Assembly, to the Convention at Philadelphia. For the gloomy prospect still admits one ray of hope, that those, who began, carried on & consummated the revolution, can yet rescue America from the impending ruin.

—Washington Papers, Library of Congress. Enclosed with his letter, Randolph sent a printed copy of the 23 November 1786 act authorizing the appointment of delegates to the Constitutional Convention and transcripts of the journals of the House of Delegates and Senate in which Washington and six others were elected to the Convention. Washington wrote to Governor Randolph declining the appointment on 21 December. On 4 January 1787 the Governor, with the Executive Council's concurrence, wrote Washington again entreating him "not to decide on a refusal immediately."

# *Washington Must Attend*

## James Madison to George Washington, Richmond, 7 December 1786

Notwithstanding the communications in your favor of the 18th. Ult: which has remained till now to be acknowledged, it was the opinion of every judicious friend whom I consulted that your name could not be spared from the Deputation to the Meeting in May in Philada. It was supposed that in the first place, the peculiarity of the mission and its acknowledged pre-eminence over every other public object, may possibly reconcile your undertaking it, with the respect which is justly due & which you wish to pay to the late officers of the army; and in the second place that although you should find that or any other consideration an obstacle to your attendance on the service, the advantage of having your name in the front of the appointment as a mark of the earnestness of Virginia, and an invitation to the most select characters from every part of the Confederacy, ought at all events to be made use of. In these sentiments I own I fully concurred, and flatter myself that they will at least apologize for my departure from those held out in your letter. I even flatter myself that they will merit a serious consideration with yourself, whether the difficulties which you enumerate ought not to give way to them. . . .

—Washington Papers, Library of Congress.

# The Principal Reason for Not Attending

芝芝

GEORGE WASHINGTON TO JAMES MADISON,
MOUNT VERNON, 16 DECEMBER 1786

. . . Besides the reasons which are assigned in my circular letter to the several State Societies of the Cincinnati, for my non-attendance at the next General Meeting to be holden in Philadelphia the first Monday of May, there exists one of a political nature, which operates more forceably on my mind than all the others;—and which, in confidence, I will now communicate to you.—

When this Society was first formed, I am persuaded not a member of it conceived that it would give birth to those Jealousies, or be chargeable with those dangers (real or imaginary) with which the minds of many, & some of respectable characters, were filled.—The motives which induced the Officers to enter into it were, I am confident, truly & frankly recited in the Institution: one of which, indeed the principal; was to establish a charitable fund for the Relief of such of their compatriots—the Widows—and dependants of them—as were fit subjects for their support; & for whom no public provision had been made.—But the trumpet being sounded, the alarm was spreading far & wide; I readily perceived therefore that unless a modification of the plan could be effected (—to anihilate the Society altogether was impracticable, on acct. of the foreign Officers who had been admitted)—that irritations wd. arise which would soon draw a line betn. the Society, & their fellow Citizens.—To prevent this.—To conciliate the affections—And to convince the World of the purity of the plan—I exerted myself, and with much difficulty, effected the changes which appeared in the Recommendation from the General Meeting to those of the States; the accomplishment of which was not easy; & I have since heard, that whilst some States acceded to the recommendation, others are not disposed thereto, alledging that, unreasonable prejudices and ill founded jealousies ought not to influence a measure laudable in its institution, & salutary in its objects & operation.— Under these circumstances, there will be no difficulty in conceiving, that the part I should have had to have acted, would have been delicate.—On the one hand, I might be charged with dereliction to the Officers, who had nobly supported, and had treated me with uncommon marks of attention and attachment.—On the other, with supporting a measure incompatible (some say) with republican principles. I thought it best therefore without assigning this (the principal reason) to decline the Presidency, and to excuse my attendance at the meeting on the ground, which is firm & just; the necessity of paying attention to my private concerns;—to conformity to my determination of passing the remainder of my days in a state of retirement—and to indisposition; occasioned by Rheumatick complaints with which, at times, I am a good deal afflicted.—Professing at the sametime my entire approbation of the institution as altered, and the pleasure I feel at the subsidence of those Jealousies which yielded to the change.—Presuming, on the general adoption of them.

I have been thus particular to shew, that under circumstances like these, I should feel myself in an awkward situation to be in Philadelphia on another public occasion during the sitting of this Society.—That the prest. æra is pregnant of great, & *strange* events, none who will cast their eyes around them, can deny.—What may be brought forth between this and the first of May to remove the difficulties which at present labour in my Mind, against the acceptance of the honor which has lately been conferred on me by the Assembly, is not for me to predict; but I should think it incompatible with that candour which ought to characterize an honest mind, not to declare that under my present view of the matter, I should be too much embarrassed by the meetings of these two bodies in the same place, in the same moment (after what I have written) to be easy in the situation;—and consequently, that it wd. be improper to let my appointment stand in the way of any other.

Of this, you who have had the whole matter fully before you, will judge; for having received no other than private intimation of my election, and unacquainted with the formalities which are, or ought to be used on these occasions, silence may be deceptious, or considered as disrespectful;—The imputation of both, or either, I would wish to avoid.—This is the cause of the present disclosure, immediately on the receipt of your letter, which has been locked up by Ice; for I have had no communication with Alexandria for many days, till the day before yesterday. . . .

—Rosenbach Museum, Philadelphia.

# Keeping the Door Open

☙ ☙

JAMES MADISON TO GEORGE WASHINGTON,
RICHMOND, 24 DECEMBER 1786

Your favour of the 16th. inst: came to hand too late on thursday evening to be answered by the last mail. I have considered well the circumstances which it confidentially discloses, as well as those contained in your preceding favor. The difficulties which they oppose to an acceptance of the appointment in which you are included can as little be denied, as they can fail to be regretted. But I still am inclined to think that the posture of our affairs, if it should continue, would prevent every criticism on the situation which the cotemporary meetings would place you in; and wish that at least a door could be kept open for your acceptance hereafter, in case the gathering clouds should become so dark and menacing as to supercede every consideration, but that of our national existence or safety. A suspence of your ultimate determination would be no wise inconvenient in a public view, as the Executive are authorized to fill vacancies and can fill them at any time, and in any event three out of seven deputies are authorized to represent the State. How far it may be admissible in another view, will depend perhaps in some measure on the chance of your finally undertaking the service; but principally on the correspondence which is now passing on the subject between yourself and the Governour....

—Washington Papers, Library of Congress.

# "A Remedy for the Disorders of the Body Politic"

※ ※

## HENRY KNOX TO GEORGE WASHINGTON, NEW YORK, 14 JANUARY 1787

. . . You ask what prevented the eastern states from attending the September meeting at Annapolis?[1]

It is difficult to give a precise answer to this question—perhaps torpidity in New Hampshire, Faction, and heats about their paper money in Rhode Island & jealousy in Connecticut—Massachusetts had chosen delegates to attend, who did not decline untill very late, and the finding other persons to supply their places, was attended with delay so that the convention had broken up, by the time the new chosen delegates reached Philadelphia.

With respect to the convention proposed to meet in May, there are different sentiments—some suppose it an irregular assembly, unauthorized by the confederation, which points out the mode by which any alterations shall be made. Others suppose, that the proposed convention would be totally inadequate to our situation, unless it should make an appeal to the people of every State, and a request, to call state conventions of the people, for the sole purpose of choosing delegates to represent them in a general convention of all the United States, to consider, revise, amend, or change the federal system in such a manner, as to them should seem meet, and to publish the same for general Observance, without any reference to the parts or states for acceptance or confirmation—were this mode prac-

---

[1] The Annapolis Convention met from 11 to 14 September 1786.

ticable it would certainly be the most summary, and if the choice of delegates was judicious, in proportion to its importance, it might be the most eligible—There are others who are of opinion that Congress ought to take up the defects of the present system, point them out to the respective Legislatures, and recommend certain alterations—

The recommendations of Congress are attended with so little effect, that any alterations by that means seem to be a hopeless business—Indeed every expedient which can be proposed, conditioned on a reference back to the Legislatures, or state conventions seems to be of the same nature.

Some gentlemen are apprehensive that a convention of the nature proposed to meet in May next, might devise some expedients to brace up, the present defective confederation so as just to serve to keep us together, while it would prevent, those exertions for a national character, which is essential to our happiness—that in this point of view, it might be attended with the bad effect, of assisting us to creep on in our present miserable condition, without a hope of a generous constitution, that should at once shield us from the effects of faction and despotism—

You will see by this sketch my dear sir how various are the opinions of men—and how difficult it will be to bring them to concur in any effective government—I am persuaded, if you were determined to attend the convention, and it should be generally known, it would induce the eastern states to send delegates to it. I should therefore be much obliged for information of your decision on this subject—At the same time the principles of the purest and most respectful friendship, induce me to say, that however strongly I wish for measures which would lead to national happiness and glory, yet I do not wish you to be concerned in any political operations, of which, there are such various opinions. There may indeed, arise some solemn occasion, in which you may conceive it to be your duty again to exert your utmost talents for to promote the happiness of your Country. But this occasion must be of an unequivocal nature in which the enlightened and virtuous citizens should generally concur.

Notwithstanding the contrary opinions respecting the proposed convention, were I to presume to give my own judgement, it would be in favor of the convention, and I sincerely hope that it may be generally attended—I do not flatter myself that the public mind is so sufficiently informed and harmonized as that an effective government would be adopted by the convention, and proposed to the United States, or that if this were practicable, that the people of the several states, are sufficiently prepared to receive it.—But it seems to be highly important that some object should be held forth to the people as a remedy for the disorders of the body politic—were this done by so respectable a set of men as those to be sent to the convention, even if it were not so perfect in the first instance, as it might be afterwards, yet it would be a stage in the business, and men's minds would be exerted on the subject and appreciated towards a good Constitution—were strong events to arise between this and the time of meeting, enforcing the necessity of a vigorous government, it should be a preparation which might be embraced by the convention to propose at once an efficient system—

Although it may be confessed that a convention originating from the respective Legislatures instead of the people themselves, is not the regular mode pointed out by the confederation, yet as our system in the opinion of men of reflection is so very defective, it may reasonably be doubted, whether the constitutional mode of amendment, would be adequate to our critical situation—if on an examination this should be found to be the case, the proposed convention may be the best expedient that could be devised—unrestrained by forms, it would be able to consider every proposition fully,

and decide agreably to the sentiments of the majority—
But in a body constituted as Congress is, a single member frequently may frustrate, the opinions of 17/18ths
of the United States assembled by representation in that
body—There are a variety of other reasons which in
my mind have the influence to induce a preference for
the convention—but the different opinions about it, will
probably prevent a general attendance.

In my former letters I mentioned that men of reflection and principle were tired of the imbecilities of
the present government—but I did not point out any
substitute. It would be important to form the plan of
a new house before we pull down the old one—The
subject has not been sufficiently discussed, as yet in
public to decide precisely on the form of the edifice.
It is out of all question that the foundation, must be of
republican principles, but so modified and wrought together, that whatever shall be erected thereon, should
be durable, & efficient. I speak entirely of the federal
government, or what would be better one *government*
instead of an association of governments—were it possible to effect, a general government of this kind it
might be constituted of an assembly, or lower house,
chosen for one two or three years, a senate chosen for
five six or seven years, and the executive under the title
of Governor General chosen by the assembly and senate, for the term of seven years, but liable to an impeachment of the lower house, and triable by the senate—A judicial to be appointed by the Governor General
during good behaviour, but impeachable by the lower
house and triable by the senate. The laws passed by
the general governmt. to be obeyed by the local governments, and if necessary to be enforced by a body
of armed men to be kept for the purposes which should
be designated—All national objects, to be designed and
executed by the general government, without any reference to the local governments. This rude sketch is
considered as the government of the least possible pow-

ers to preserve the confederated governments—To attempt to establish less will be to hazard the existence of republicanism, and to subject us, either to a division of the European powers, or to a despotism arising from high handed commotions—

I have thus my dear sir obeyed what seemed to be your desire, and given you the ideas which have presented themselves from reflection, and the opinions of others.—May heaven direct us to the best means for the dignity, and Happiness of the United States....

—Washington Papers, Library of Congress.

# *America's Last Stake to Play*

✗ ✗

DAVID HUMPHREYS TO GEORGE WASHINGTON, NEW HAVEN, 20 JANUARY 1787

I am indeed much flattered by the private and confidential communications contained in your favor of the 26 of Dec.—I trust; on the present critical & momentous occasion, by disclosing the very sentiments of my soul without reservation; I shall not render myself less deserving of your confidence; or worthy a place in your friendship. . . .

As to a Convention, it has not until lately engrossed but little share in the conversation here. I am induced to expect the only good it can do, will be to demonstrate to the People, that a number of characters in whom they repose confidence, believe seriously we cannot remain as a nation much longer, in the present manner of administering our actual Government. The evil appears to me to consist more in the untowardly dispositions of the States, (who make no hesitation in palpably violating the Confederacy whenever it suits their interest) rather than in the form of our national Compact as it exists on paper. What is to be done to cure these dispositions? We may have what forms we please, but without coertion, they are idle as the wind. Now let us enquire what effect may probably be produced from the Convention. In the first place there is a diversity of sentiment respecting the legality & expediency of such a Meeting: Those who are opposed to the measure say there cannot be a full representation of the People for revising the Confœderation, because the freemen at large have not been consulted in any instance; and because the Legislatures who appoint Deputies, are not authorised by their Constituents to make such appointment. They suppose a Convention to be an interference with, if not an usurpation of the functions of Congress, and that, if any recommendations are to go to the People, they should originate with Congress. But neither of these is the reason, why those members of our Assembly, who are perfectly fœderal in their policy, did not urge that the subject should have been taken up & an appointment made. The reason was, a conviction that the persons who would be elected; were some of the most antifœderal men in the State, who believe or act as if they believed that Congress is already possessed of too unlimited powers, and who would wish, apparently, to see the Union dissolved. These Demagogues really affect to persuade the people (to use their own phraseology) that they are only in danger of having their liberties stolen away, by an artful, designing Aristocracy. This jealousy, I perceive, exists in some other Governments. I do not learn that Commissioners have been appointed from all of the New England States. Some of the Assemblies will not convene before May, unless called on extraordinary emergency. To that it is almost certain that the

Convention will be but partial in point of representation. But should it be compleat, and should the members be unanimous in recommending, in the most forcible, the most glowing, the most pathetic terms which language can afford, that it is indispenable to the salvation of the Country, Congress should be cloathed with more ample powers.—I am as confident as I am of my own existence, the States will not all comply with the recommendation. They have a mortal reluctance to divest themselves of the smallest attribute of independent; seperate Sovereignty. The personal character of yourself & some other Gentlemen would have a weight on individuals—but on democratic Assemblies & the bulk of the People, your opinions & your eloquence would be "triffles light as air." After the abominable neglects, with which your recommendations of the Army have been treated; he must indeed have faith to remove mountains, who can believe in the good dispositions of the Country. We are already nearly ruined by believing too much—We have believed that the Citizens of the United States were better than the rest of the world; and that they could be managed in Society without compulsion.

In effect, I conceive that, if the Confœderation should not meet with a speedy dissolution, Congress must & will gradually & imperceptably acquire the habits & the means of enforcing their dicisions—But if the people have not wisdom or virtue enough to govern themselves, or what is the same thing to suffer themselves to be governed by men of their own election; why then I must think it is in vain to struggle against the torrent, it is in vain to strive to compel mankind to be happy & free contrary to their inclination. The inability, in that case, or rather their jealous & factious Leaders will produce a crisis of a different nature. All that Patriots & good men can do, will be to await events, to foresee as far as may be, & make the best of them.

I have dilated thus largely on the general subject,

to shew that I concur fully in sentiment with you, concerning the inexpediency of your attending the Convention. This is also the decided opinion of our friend Colo. Trumbull,[1] with whom I have been since the receipt of your letter on purpose to take his advice (he begs his best respects may be presented to you).

As to your particular & private reasons against attending, they are clearly sufficient to convince any reasonable man of the propriety & *consistency* of your conduct.

1st. You declared, on resigning your Commission that you would not interfere again with public affairs.—Should a period eventually arrive & probably it may) when this declaration ought to be dispensed with: that Crisis is certainly not yet come.

2ndly. You may urge with peculiar propriety Your private affairs, & a right to enjoy the remainder of life in tranquillity.

3dly. You have happily excused yourself, for substantial reasons, from attending the General Meeting of the Cincinnati.—This ought to be considered as an additional apology. Your declining to attend that Meeting, will not (under the present circumstances) be considered in an unfavorable light by any discription of Men.—But should you afterwards attend the Convention, it would more than probably produce uneasiness among the Officers in general, & evidently give an occasion to a certain Class to represent your conduct as influenced by ambition on one hand; & as discovering a derilection of your old friends, on the other.

4thly. The result of the Convention may not be perhaps so important as is expected: in which case your character would be materially affected. Other people can work up the present scene. I know your personal influence & character, is, justly considered, the last

[1]John Trumbull of Lebanon, Conn., had been secretary to General Washington from 1781 to 1783.

stake which America has to play.—Should you not reserve yourself for the united call of a Continent entire?

5thly. If you should attend on this Convention & concur in recommending measures, which should be generally adopted, but opposed in some parts of the Union; it would doubtless be understood that you had, in a degree, pledged yourself for their execution.—This would at once sweep you back, irretreivably, into the tide of public affairs.

One feels such a lassitude & inaccuracy in attempting to unbosom himself in writing, as makes him much less explicit & clear than he would be in an oral communication. Was I only at a moderate distance, I should endeavour to communicate verbally many sentiments respecting circumstances & characters, which must now be suppressed. . . .

—Washington Papers, Library of Congress.

# A Tumbled and Tossed Political Machine

茭 茭

GEORGE WASHINGTON TO HENRY KNOX,
MOUNT VERNON, 3 FEBRUARY 1787

I feel myself exceedingly obliged to you for the full and friendly communications in your letters of the 14th. 21st. and 25th. Ulto; and shall (critically as matters are described in the latter) be exceedingly anxious to know the issue of the movements of the forces that were assembling in support of, and in opposition to the Constitution of Massachusetts. The moment is important!—

If government shrinks or is unable to enforce its Laws, Fresh Manœuvres will be displayed by the insurgents—anarchy and confusion Must prevail—and every thing will be turned topsy turvey in that State; where it is not probable it will end.

In your letter of the 14th. you express a wish to be informed of my intention respecting the Convention proposed to be held in Philadelphia May next. In *confidence* I inform you that it is not, at this time, my intention to attend it.—When this matter *was* first moved in the Assembly of this State, some of the principal characters of it wrote to me requesting they might be permitted to put my name in the delegation—To this I objected—They again pressed, and I again refused; assigning among other reasons, my having declined meeting the Society of the Cincinnati at that place about the same time and that I thought it would be disrespectful to that body to whom I owe much, to be there on any other occasion.—Notwithstanding these intimations my name was inserted in the Act; and an official communication thereof made by the Executive to me to whom at the same time that I expressed my Sense for the confidence reposed in me, I declared that as I saw no prospect of my attending it was my wish that my name might not remain in the delegation to the exclusion of another—To this I have been requested in emphatical terms not to decide absolutely as no inconvenience would result from the non-appointment of another, at least for some time yet.—

Thus the matter stands which is the reason of my saying to you in *confidence* that at present I retain my first intention, not to go.—In the mean while as I have the fullest conviction of your friendship for and attachment to me, know your abilities to judge—and your means of information I shall receive any communications from you on this subject with thankfulness—my first wish is, to do for the best and to act with propriety. you know me too well to believe that reserve or concealment of any opinion or circumstance would be at all agreeable to me. The legallity of this Convention I do not mean to discuss—nor how problematical the issue of it may be.—That powers are wanting, none can deny.—through what medium they are to be derived will, like other matters, engage the attention of the wise—that which takes the shortest course to obtain them, in my opinion will under present circumstances be found best—otherwise, like a house on fire whilst the most regular mode of extinguishing the flames is contended for, the building's reduced to Ashes.—My opinion of the energetic wants of the fœderal government are well known: my public annunciations and private declarations have uniformly *expressed* these sentiments and however constitutionally it may be for Congress to point out the defects of the fœderal system, I am strongly inclined to believe that it would not be found the most efficatious channel for the recommendation, more especially the alterations to flow for reasons too obvious to enumerate.—

The System on which you seem disposed to build a National government, is certainly more energetic, and dare say in every point of view is more desirable than the Present, which from experience we find is not only slow, debilitated, and liable to be thwarted by every breath, but is defective in that secrecy, which for the accomplishment of many of the most important National objects is indispensably necessary, and besides, having the Legislative, Executive and Judiciary departments concentered is exceptionable.[1]—But at the same time that I give this opinion, I believe the political Machine will yet be much tumbled and tossed, and possibly be wrecked altogether, before that or any thing like it will be adopted.—The darling sovereignties of

[1]The Articles of Confederation provided for no separate executive or judiciary. A single-house Congress controlled the legislative, executive, and judicial powers.

each State—the Governors elected, and elect—the Legislators—with a long tribe of etceteras whose political
importance will be lessened if not annihilated, would
give their Weight of opposition to such a Revolution
but I may be speaking without book for scarcely ever
going off my own farms, I see few people who do not
call upon me and am very little acquainted with the
sentiments of the Great public; indeed, after what I
have seen or rather after what I have heard I shall be
surprized at nothing for if 3 years since, any person
had told me that their would have been such formidable
rebellion as exists at this day against the Laws and
Constitutions of our own making I should have thought
him a bedlamite, a fit subject for a mad House.

—Letterbook, Washington Papers, Library of Congress.

## Seeking Advice

䒑 䒑

### GEORGE WASHINGTON TO HENRY KNOX, MOUNT VERNON, 8 MARCH 1787

. . . I am glad to hear that Congress are about to
remove some of the stumbling blocks which lay in the
way of the proposed Convention.[1]—A Convention I
wish to see tried—after which, if the present government is not efficient, conviction of the propriety of a
change will dissiminate through every rank, and class
of people and may be brought about in place—till which,
however necessary it may appear in the eyes of the

[1] On 21 February 1787 Congress sanctioned a constitutional convention to meet in Philadelphia.

more discerning, my opinion is, that it cannot be effected without great contention, and much confusion.— It is among the evils, and perhaps is not the smallest, of democratical governments, that the people must *feel*, before they will *see*.—When this happens, they are roused to action—hence it is that this form of government is so slow.—I am indirectly, and delicately pressed to attend this convention.—Several reasons are opposed to it in my mind, and not the least my having declined attending the General Meeting of the Cincinnati, which is to be holden in Philadelphia at the same time on account of the disrespect it might *seem* to offer to that Society, to be there on another occasion.—A thought however has lately run through my mind, which is attended with embarrassment.—It is, whether my non-attendance in this Convention will not be considered as a deriliction to republicanism—nay more—whether other motives may not (however injuriously) be ascribed to me for not exerting myself on this occasion in support of it.—Under these circumstances let me pray you, my dear Sir, to inform me confidentially, what the public expectation is on this head.—that is, whether I will, or ought to be there?—You are much in the way of obtaining this knowledge, and I can depend upon your friendship—candour—and judgment in the communication of it, as far as it shall appear to you.—My final determination (if what I have already given to the Executive of this State is not considered in that light) cannot be delayed beyond the time necessary for your reply.

—Sol Feinstone Collection of the American Revolution, no. 2160, American Philosophical Society, Philadelphia. Washington wrote a similar letter to David Humphreys on the same day.

# "The Last Anchor
of Our Hope"

✠ ✠

GOV. EDMUND RANDOLPH TO GEORGE WASHINGTON,
RICHMOND, 11 MARCH 1787

I must call upon your friendship to excuse me for again mentioning the convention at Philadelphia. Your determination having been fixed on a thorough review of your situation, I feel, like an intruder, when I again hint a wish, that you could join the delegation. But every day brings forth some new crisis, and the confederation [i.e., the Convention] is, I fear, the last anchor of our hope. Congress have taken up the subject, and appointed the second monday in May next, as the day of meeting. Indeed from my private correspondence I doubt whether the existence of that body even thro' this year may not be questionable under our present circumstances.

—Washington Papers, Library of Congress.

# Doubly Earned:
## "The Father of Your Country"

※ ※

HENRY KNOX TO GEORGE WASHINGTON,
NEW YORK, 19 MARCH 1787

... I have the satisfaction of acknowledging the receipt of your favor of the 8th which I received on the 17th instant. ...

The opinion of Congress respecting the proposed convention has had good effects. It is now highly probable that the convention will be general. All the States have already chosen delegates to attend it, excepting Rhode-Island and Connecticut, and there can be but little doubt of their making a seasonable choice.

Your observations in favor of the experiment of a convention are conclusive—Our present federal government is indeed a name, a shadow, without power or effect. We must either have a government of the same materials, differently constructed, or we must have a government of events.

But should the convention possess the magnanimity to propose a wise modification of a national government, without regarding the present local and contracted views, that the mass of the people in the respective States entertain of the subject leaving to time, better information, and events to ripen their judgements, much, much might be hoped. But if only propositions be obtained for bracing up the present radically defective thing, so as to enable us to drag on with pain and labor, for a few years, then better had it been, that the idea of the convention had never been conceived.

As you have thought proper my dear Sir, to request my opinion respecting your attendance at the convention, I shall give it with the utmost sincerity and frankness.

I imagine that your own satisfaction or chagrin and that of your friends will depend entirely on the result of the convention—For I take it for granted that however reluctantly you may acquiesce, that you will be constrained to accept of the president's Chair. Hence the proceedings of the convention will more immediately be appropriated to you than to any other person—

Were the convention to propose only amendments and patch work to the present defective confederation, Your reputation would in a degree suffer—But were an energetic, and judicious system to be proposed under Your signature, it would be a circumstance highly honorable to your fame, in the judgement of the present and future ages; and doubly entitle you to the glorious republican epithet—The Father of Your Country.

But the men generally chosen, being of the first information, great reliance may be placed on the wisdom and vigor of their Councils and judgement, and therefore the balance of my opinion preponderates greatly in favor of your attendance.

I am persuaded that your name has had already great influence to induce the States to come into the measure—That your attendance will be grateful, and your absence chagrining—That your presence would confer on the assembly a national complexion, and that it would more than any other circumstance induce a compliance to the propositions of the convention. . . .

—Washington Papers, Library of Congress.

# Advised to Stay Away

⚔ ⚔

DAVID HUMPHREYS TO GEORGE WASHINGTON,
NEW HAVEN, 24 MARCH 1787

I have but just had the pleasure to receive your two favours of the 18th of Feby and 8th instant—Nor will I delay a moment giving my sentiments on the subject of the latter, for the sake of throwing them into a more elegant dress or methodical arrangement. I need hardly preface my observations by saying, that I feel myself superlatively happy in your confidential communications, and in opportunities of proving that I do not write for the purpose of acquiring a reputation for fine composition, but for the sake of justifying the favourable opinion you have been pleased to form of my attachment & sincerity.

I may then with justice assert that so far from having seen any reason to change my opinion respecting the inexpediency of your attending the Convention in May next, additional arguments have occurred to confirm me in the sentiment. The probability, which existed when I wrote before, that nothing general or effectual would be done by the Convention, amounts now almost to a certainty. For the Assembly of Rhode Island (as I am lately given to understand) have decided against sending any Representation. Connecticut is under the influence of a few such miserable, narrowminded & I may say wicked Politicians, that I question very much whether the Legislature will chuse Members to appear in the Convention; and if they do, my apprehension is still greater that they will be sent on purpose to impede any salutary measures that might be proposed. That there is little doubt, is actually the case with N. York, as it is asserted, two out of their three Delegates are directly antifœderal. What chance is there, then that entire unanimity will prevail?[1] Should this be the fact, however, would not the several Members, as it were, pledge themselves for the execution of their system? And would not this inevitably launch you again on a sea of Politics? As you justly observe matters must probably grow worse before they will be better.

Since I had the honour of addressing you last on this subject, I have been in the way of hearing the speculations of many different Characters on the proposed Convention, and their conjectures on the part you would act in consequence of your appointment to it. I have heard few express any sanguine expectations concerning the successful issue of the Meeting, & I think not one has judged it eligible for you to attend.

In this part of the Union, your not attending will not be considered either by the fœderal, or antifœderal party, as a dereliction of Republicanism. The former believe it unimportant, or perhaps, injurious, to the national Interests for you to come forward at present—the latter look upon the Convention as rather intended to subvert than support Republicanism: and will readily excuse your Non-attendance.

Notwithstanding your circular letter to the Cincinnati, I think it probable the General Meeting will re-elect you President—I hope they will—for matters, I am confident, will in some way or another work right before all is over.

Congress appear to be in a state of mortal stupefaction or lethargy. . . .

—Washington Papers, Library of Congress.

[1]The Articles of Confederation required the unanimous ratification of the state legislatures to adopt amendments.

# "A Resolution to Go"

✠ ✠

GEORGE WASHINGTON TO GOV. EDMUND RANDOLPH,
MOUNT VERNON, 28 MARCH 1787

Your favor of the 11th. did not come to my hand till the 24th, and since then, till now, I have been too much indisposed to acknowledge the Receipt of it.—To what cause to ascribe the detention of the letter I know not, as I never omit sending once, and often twice a week, to the post office in Alexandria.

It was the decided intention of the letter I had the honor of writing to your Excellency the 21st of December last to inform you that it was not convenient for me to attend the Convention proposed to be holden in Philadelphia in May next.—and I had entertained hope, that an other had been, or soon would be appointed in my place, in as much as it is not only inconvenient for me to leave home, but because there will be, I apprehend, too much cause to arraign my conduct with inconsistency, in again appearing on a public theater, after a public declaration to the contrary, and because it will, I fear, have a tendency to sweep me back into the tide of public affairs, when retirement and ease is so essentially necessary for, and is so much desired by me.—

However, as my friends, with a degree of sollicitude which is unusual, seem to wish my attendance on this occasion; I have come to a resolution to go, if my health will permit, provided, from the lapse of time between the date of your Excellency's letter and this reply the Executive may not (the reverse of which would be highly pleasing to me) have turned their thoughts to some other character for independently of all other considerations, I have of late, been so much afflicted

77

with a Rheumatic complaint in my shoulder that at times I am hardly able to raise my hand to my head or turn myself in bed.—This consequently might prevent my attendance—and eventually, a representation of the State, which would afflict me more sinsibly than the disorder that occasioned it.

If after the expression of these sentiments, the Executive should consider me as one of the delegates, I would thank your Excellency for the earliest advice of it, because, if I am able, and should go to Philadelphia, I shall have some previous arrangement to make, and would set off for that place the first, or second day of May, that I may be there in time to account personally for my conduct to the General Meeting of the Cincinnati which is to convene on the first Monday of that Month.—My feelings would be much hurt if that body should, otherwise ascribe my attending the one and not on the other occasion to a disrespectful inattention to the Society, when the fact is that I shall ever retain the most lively and affectionate regard for the Members of which it is composed, on account of their attachment to, and uniform support of me upon many trying occasions, as well as on account of their public virtues, patriotism and sufferings.

I hope your Excellency will be found among the *attending* Delegates.—I should be glad to be informed who the others are.—and cannot conclude without once more and in emphatical terms, praying that if there is not a *decided* Representation in *prospect* without me, that another may be chosen in my room without ceremony, and without delay; for the reason already assigned; for it would be unfortunate indeed, if the State which was the mover of this Convention, should be unrepresented in it—

—Letterbook, Washington Papers, Library of Congress.

# "No Temporising Expedient"

⚔ ⚔

GEORGE WASHINGTON TO JAMES MADISON,
MOUNT VERNON, 31 MARCH 1787

... I am glad to find that Congress have recommended to the States to appear in the Convention proposed to be holden in Philadelphia in May. I think the reasons in favor, have the preponderancy of those against the measure. It is idle in my opinion to suppose that the Sovereign [i.e., Congress] can be insensible of the inadequacy of the powers under which it acts—and that seeing, it should not recommend a revision of the Fœderal system, when it is considered by many as the *only* Constitutional mode by which the defects can be remedied. Had Congress proceeded to a delineation of the Powers, it might have sounded an alarm—but as the case is, I do not conceive that it will have that effect. . . .

I am fully of opinion that those who lean to a Monarchical governmt. have either not consulted the public mind, or that they live in a region where the levelling principles in which they were bred, being entirely irradicated, is much more productive of Monarchical ideas than are to be found in the Southern States, where from the habitual distinctions which have always existed among the people, one would have expected the first generation, and the most rapid growth of them. I also am clear, that even admitting the utility;—nay necessity of the form—yet that the period is not arrived for adopting the change without shaking the Peace of this Country to its foundation.

That a thorough reform of the present system is indispensable, none who have capacities to judge will deny and with hand and heart I hope the business will be essayed in a full Convention. After which, if more powers, and more decision is not found in the existing form—If it still wants energy and that secresy and dispatch (either from the non-attendance, or the local views of its members) which is characteristick of good Government—And if it shall be found (the contrary of which however I have always been more affrd. of, than of the abuse of them) that Congress will upon all proper occasions exercise the powers with a firm and steady hand, instead of frittering them back to the Individual States where the members in place of viewing themselves in their National character, are too apt to be looking—I say after this essay is made if the system proves inefficient, conviction of the necessity of a change will be dissiminated among all classes of the People. Then, and not till then, in my opinion can it be attempted without involving all the evils of civil discord. . . .

It gives me pleasure to hear that there is a probability of a full Representation of the States in Convention, but if the delegates come to it under fetters, the salutary ends proposed will in my opinion be greatly embarrassed & retarded, if not altogether defeated. I am anxious to know how this matter really is, as my wish is, that the Convention may adopt no temporising expedient, but probe the defects of the Constitution to the bottom, and provide radical cures, whether they are agreed to or not. A conduct like this, will stamp wisdom and dignity on the proceedings, and be looked to as a luminary, which sooner or later will shed its influence. . . .

—Emmet Collection, New York Public Library.

# The American
# Fabius Arrives

⚔ ⚔

On the coming of the AMERICAN FABIUS to the Federal Convention in May next.

*Had not great Cromwell aim'd to gain a crown,*
*Unsullied tales would hand his mem'ry down.*
The hero comes, each voice resound his praise
No envious shafts can dare to chill his rays;
All hail! great man! who for thy country's cause,
Flew at her call for to protect the laws.
But while dull notes like these my song disarm'd,
His rigid virtues ev'ry patriot warm'd;
Inspir'd each leader at his standard met,
*Laurens*[1] who fell, with *Greene* and *La Fayette.*
Like the fair structure on the river side,
Which from reflection dazzles on the tide,
Each caught the flame, celestial pow'rs unite,
And stimulate them on to aid the fight.
He fought, he won, and calm'd the raging storm,
Tho' rais'd by pride abstruse, in fury's form;
Thy unambitious steps will paint thy name
To future ages thro' historic fame.
Columbia now with independence crown'd,
Proclaims her consequence on foreign ground.
For, oh! great WASHINGTON! while war did rage,
From *Clinton* retrospectively to *Gage,*[2]

[1]John Laurens, Washington's aide in 1777 and special envoy to France in 1780, was killed in a minor skirmish with the British in August 1782.
[2]British commanders Henry Clinton and Thomas Gage.

81

Stood firm—till peace did crown thy native shore,
By superceding war's terrific roar.
    A time of rest at length appear'd in view,
With all its happiness in blooming hue;
A calm which oft the hero wish'd to see,
Where rural blessings with his mind agree;
But fly once more the *Senate* house to grace,
And crown the States with everlasting peace.

ALEXIS.

    Philadelphia, April 6, 1787.

—Philadelphia *Independent Gazetteer*, 9 April 1787. By 21 May this poem was reprinted eight times: twice in New York and once each in Pennsylvania, Connecticut, Massachusetts, Rhode Island, New Hampshire and South Carolina.

# *"Sages and Patriots"*

Reasonably is it to be expected, says a correspondent—that the deliberations of the sages and patriots, who are to meet in Convention at Philadelphia, next month, will be attended with much good—An union of the abilities of so distinguished a body of men, among whom will be a FRANKLIN and a WASHINGTON, cannot but produce the most salutary measures.—These last names affixed to their recommendations (and it is to be hoped that this will be the case) will stamp a confidence in them, which the narrow-soul'd, antifederal politicians in the several States, who, by their influence, have hith-

erto damn'd us a nation, will not dare to attack, or
endeavour to nullify.

—*Massachusetts Centinel*, 14 April 1787. By 2 June this paragraph was reprinted thirteen times: three times each in
New Hampshire, Massachusetts, and Pennsylvania, and
once each in Vermont, Rhode Island, Connecticut, and
New York.

# Welcomed by Bells

Yesterday His Excellency General WASHINGTON, a
member of the grand convention, arrived here [Phil-
adelphia].—He was met at some distance and escorted
into the city by the troop of horse, and saluted at his
entrance by the artillery. The joy of the people on the
coming of this great and good man was shown by their
acclamations and the ringing of bells.

—*Pennsylvania Packet*, 14 May 1787. By 30 June thirty-one
newspapers throughout the country reprinted this account.

# Hailed Along the Way

We have the pleasure to announce the arrival of
General Washington on Sunday last, who was met and
escorted into this city by the troop of light horse. Notwithstanding the badness of the weather great numbers
of respectable citizens assembled in the streets to hail
him as he passed, and universal satisfaction was com-

municated upon finding our old and faithful commander in the full enjoyment of his health and fame.

—*Pennsylvania Herald*, 16 May 1787. Eight reprints of this
account were reprinted by the end of June.

# Obedience to the Voice of God and Country

毕 毕

## HARRINGTON: TO THE FREEMEN OF THE UNITED STATES

... To beget confidence in, and an attachment to,
a new fœderal government, let us attend to the characters of the men who are met to form it.

Many of them were members of the first Congress,
that sat in Philadelphia in the year 1774.

Many of them were part of that band of patriots,
who, with halters round their necks, signed the declaration of independence on the 4th of July, 1776.

Many of them were distinguished in the field, and
some of them bear marks of the wounds they received
in our late contest for liberty.

Perhaps no age or country ever saw more wisdom,
patriotism and probity united in a single assembly, than
we now behold in the convention of the states.

Who can read or hear, that the immortal WASHING-
TON has again quitted his beloved retirement, and obeyed
the voice of God and his country, by accepting the
chair of this illustrious body of patriots and heroes, and
doubt of the safety and blessings of the government we
are to receive from their hands?

Or who can read or hear of Franklin, Dickinson, Rutledge, R. Morris, Livingston, Randolph, Gerry, Shearman, Mifflin, Clymer, Pinkney, Read, and many others that might be mentioned, whose names are synonimous with liberty and fame, and not long to receive from them the precious ark, that is to preserve and transmit to posterity the freedom of America?

Under the present weak, imperfect and distracted government of Congress, anarchy, poverty, infamy, and SLAVERY, await the United States.

Under such a government as will probably be formed by the present convention, America may yet enjoy peace, safety, liberty and glory.

*—Pennsylvania Gazette* and also the *Pennsylvania Journal* on 30 May 1787. By 11 August, "Harrington" was reprinted thirty-one times throughout the country. "Harrington" was written by Benjamin Rush, a Philadelphia physician.

# *Inability to Resist the Call*

🏹 🏹

GEORGE WASHINGTON TO MARQUIS DE LAFAYETTE, PHILADELPHIA, 6 JUNE 1787

... You will I dare say, be surprized my dear Marquis to receive a letter from me at this place,—you will probably, be more so, when you hear that I am again brought, contrary to my public declaration, and intention, on a public theatre—such is the viscissitude of human affairs, and such the frailty of human nature that no man I conceive can well answer for the resolutions he enters into.—

The pressure of the public voice was so loud, I

could not resist the call to a convention of the States which is to determine whether we are to have a Government of respectability under which life, liberty, and property will be secured to us, or are to submit to one which may be the result of chance or the moment, springing perhaps from anarchy and Confusion, and dictated perhaps by some aspiring demagogue who will not consult the interest of his Country so much as his own ambitious views.—What may be the result of the present deliberations is more than I am able, at present, if I was at liberty, to inform you, & therefore I will make this letter short, with the assurance of being more particular when I can be more satisfactory. . . .

—Letterbook, Washington Papers, Library of Congress.

# Equal to the Task

🐦 🐦

. . . The Grand Fœderal Convention it is hoped will act wisely, for on their determinations alone, and our acquiescence, depends our future happiness and prosperity; and if their lives a man equal to so arduous a task, it is a WASHINGTON!

—Petersburg *Virginia Gazette*, 26 July 1787. Reprinted seven times within a month: three times in Pennsylvania and once in each Massachusetts, Rhode Island, Maryland, and South Carolina.

# Arresting American Anarchy

※ ※

... How great (adds our correspondent) must be the satisfaction of our late worthy Commander in Chief, to be called upon a second time, by the suffrages of three millions of people, to save his sinking country?— In 1775, we beheld him at the head of the armies of America, arresting the progress of British tyranny.—In the year 1787, we behold him at the head of a chosen band of patriots and heroes, arresting the progress of American anarchy, and taking the lead in laying a deep foundation for preserving that liberty by a good government, which he had acquired for his country by his sword.—Illustrious and highly favored instrument of the blessings of Heaven to America—live—live for ever!

—*Pennsylvania Gazette*, 22 August 1787. Reprinted thirty-two times within a month.

# III

## ✠ ✠

# ANSWERING
# THE CALL

## *The Election of a President*

GEORGE WASHINGTON did not want to be the first President of the United States under the Constitution, but he realized that he had virtually no choice in the matter. The delegates to the Constitutional Convention had drafted Article II of the Constitution, establishing the executive branch, with Washington in mind; and throughout the ratification debate Americans assumed that Washington would be the first President. Under this impression, most Americans felt confident that the new government would not abuse its powers and the Constitution would be properly implemented. With Washington at the helm, Americans were, therefore, willing to adopt the new Constitution which would create a strong central government. But a sizeable minority still worried about what would happen after Washington's presidency. President Washington could be trusted, but could "President Slushington?" Even Thomas Jefferson, U.S. minister to France, had misgivings: "Our jealousy is only put to sleep by the unlimited confidence we all repose in the person to whom we all look as our president. After him inferior characters may perhaps succeed and awaken us to the danger which his merit has led us into."

Washington understood the feeling throughout

America and prepared for another call to duty. In fact, one reason why Washington remained above the fray in the ratification debate—refusing even to serve as a delegate to the Virginia ratifying convention—was to avoid the charge that he was seeking personal power and aggrandizement. Thus Washington played little public role during the ten-month struggle over ratification.

Presidential electors were chosen in January 1789. On 4 February the electors cast their ballots unanimously for Washington. The new United States Congress counted the electoral votes on 6 April and appointed Charles Thomson, longtime secretary of the Continental and Confederation congresses, to inform Washington. Arriving at Mount Vernon on 14 April, Thomson notified the General of his election, and Washington decided to leave for New York City, the capital, in two days.

Throughout March and early April, Washington had been preparing to leave his Virginia home. On 1 April he wrote Henry Knox that he felt like "a culprit who is going to the place of his execution, so unwilling am I, in the evening of a life nearly consumed in public cares, to quit a peaceful abode for an ocean of difficulties." Despite these forebodings, Washington, accompanied by Thomson and David Humphreys, set out in mid morning on 16 April for New York City and his new responsibilities. The President-elect confided his anxieties to his diary as he "bid adieu to Mount Vernon, to private life, and to domestic felicity." He left this private serenity with "the best disposition to render service to my country in obedience to its call, but with less hope of answering its expectations."

For the next week, the small company slowly moved northward. Washington had often expressed the hope that this inaugural journey would be simple and free of ceremony. Such was not possible, however. Over and over again, he was escorted into town by militia, light cavalry, and private citizens; welcomed by artillery, bells, and triumphal arches; and wined, dined, and honored with odes, music, and congratulatory addresses. He arrived in New York City on 23 April with great fanfare. Despite the acclaim, Washington still had forebodings that the scene of joy might be reversed "after all my labors to do good." But for now, Americans were optimistic. They had a new federal government, and they had their beloved General back in the service of his country.

# Called by Three Million

✠ ✠

GEORGE WASHINGTON, Esq; has already been destined, by a thousand voices, to fill the place of the first President of the United States, under the new frame of government. While the deliverers of a nation in other countries have hewn out a way to power with the sword, or seized upon it by stratagems and fraud, our illustrious Hero peaceably retired to his farm after the war, from whence it is expected he will be called, by the suffrages of three millions of people, to govern that country by his wisdom (agreeably to fixed laws) which he had previously made free by his arms.—Can Europe boast of such a man?—or can the history of the world shew an instance of such a voluntary compact between the *Deliverer* and the *delivered* of any country, as will probably soon take place in the United States.

—*Pennsylvania Gazette*, 26 September 1787. Within a month, this paragraph was reprinted forty-five times throughout the United States.

# "An Able Charioteer"

✠ ✠

GOUVERNEUR MORRIS TO GEORGE WASHINGTON, PHILADELPHIA, 30 OCTOBER 1787

... I have observed that your Name to the new Constitution has been of infinite Service. Indeed I am convinced that if you had not attended the Convention, and the same Paper had been handed out to the World, it would have met with a colder Reception, with fewer and weaker Advocates, and with more and more strenuous Opponents. As it is, should the Idea prevail that you would not accept of the Presidency it would prove fatal in many Parts. Truth is, that your great and decided Superiority leads Men willingly to put you in a Place which will not add to your personal Dignity, nor raise you higher than you already stand: but they would not willingly put any other Person in the same Situation because they feel the Elevation of others as operating (by Comparison) the Degradation of themselves. And however absurd this Idea, you will agree with me that Men must be treated as Men and not as Machines, much less as Philosophers, & least of all Things as reasonable Creatures; seeing that in Effect they reason not to direct but to excuse their Conduct

Thus much for the public Opinion on these Subjects, which must not be neglected in a Country where Opinion is every Thing. I will add my Conviction that of all Men you are best fitted to fill that Office. Your cool steady Temper is *indispensibly necessary* to give a firm and manly Tone to the new Government. To constitute a well poised political Machine is the Task of no common Workman; but to set it in Motion requires still greater Qualities. When once a-going, it will proceed a long Time from the original Impulse. Time gives to primary Institutions the mighty Power of Habit, and Custom, the Law both of Wise Men and Fools, serves as the great Commentator of human Establishments, and like other Commentators as frequently obscures as it explains the Text. No Constitution is the same on Paper and in Life. The Exercise of Authority depends on personal Character; and the Whip and Reins by which an able Charioteer governs unruly Steeds will only hurl the unskilful Presumer with more speedy & headlong Violence to the Earth. The Horses once trained may be managed by a Woman or a Child; not so when they first feel the Bit. And indeed among these thirteen Horses now about to be coupled together there are some of every Race and Character. They will listen

to your Voice, and submit to your Control; you therefore must I say *must* mount the Seat. That the Result
may be as pleasing to you as it will be useful to them
I wish but do not expect. You will however on this, as
on other Occasions, feel that interior Satisfaction &
Self Approbation which the World cannot give; and
you will have in every possible Event the Applause of
those who know you enough to respect you properly.

> —Washington Papers, Library of Congress. Morris, a thirty-
> six-year-old Philadelphia lawyer, had been a delegate to
> the Constitutional Convention. As a member of the Com-
> mittee of Style, Morris wrote the final draft of the
> Constitution.

# "You Cannot Refuse"

豪 豪

MARQUIS DE LAFAYETTE TO GEORGE WASHINGTON
PARIS, 1 JANUARY 1788

... It is Needless for me to tell You that I Read
the New Proposed Constitution With An Unspeack-
able Eagerness and Attention—I Have Admired it, and
find it is a Bold, large, and Solid frame for the Confederation—the Electionneering Principles With Respect to the Two Houses of Congress are Most Happily
Calculated—I am only Affraid of two things—1er the
Want of a declaration of Rights 2ly the Great Powers
and Possible Continuance of the President, Who May
one day or other Become a State Holder[1]—Should My
observations be well founded, I Still am Easy on two

[1]The stadtholder was the chief magistrate of Holland.

93

Accounts—The first that a Bill of Rights May Be Made if Wished for By the People Before they Accept the Constitution—My other Comfort is that You Cannot Refuse Being Elected President—and that if You think the Public Vessel Can Stir Without Such Powers, You Will Be able to lessen them, or Propose Measures Respecting the Permanence, Which Cannot fail to Insure a Greater Perfection in the Constitution, and a New Crop of Glory to Yourself—But in the Name of America, of Mankind at large, and Your Own fame, I Beseech You, my dear General, Not to deny Your Acceptance of the office of President for the first Years—You only Can Settle that Political Machine, and I foresee it Will furnish An Admirable Chapter in Your History. . . .

—Hubbard Collection, Lafayette College, Easton, Pa.

# A Concurrence of Virtues

꙰ ꙰

*To the* PEOPLE *of* AMERICA.

In the first experiment of any untried plan, every movement should be made with due caution and reflection. The office of President of the United States will probably become ere long the object of your consideration. When you shall have to determine on the man, whom you will make the first servant of a free people, it will be happy, if you shall all have previously considered the various points that should influence your choice, and all the circumstances in the situation of the favorite candidate, that may render him deserving, safe and elegible.

The first idea that presents itself to me is, that it

94

will be desirable to make the experiment with a character, whose situation prevents an attempt, by a son, to obtain the succession. Should the man of your choice have an ambitious, enterprizing son, of uncertain principles, who, forgetting at once the virtues of his father and his duty to his country, might be likely to attempt to continue in his family by lawless means the powers and honors of a President, it would be well to consider, whether the safety of the nation might not require the election of another.

Another idea which occurs is, that we be not deceived by the political character of the man himself, on whom we may desire to confer this important office. Unhappy would it be for America, if, after calling a citizen to this new and untried office, she should find that the want of occasion alone had prevented the appearance of latent seeds of fell ambition, which nature had planted in his bosom. Let us then search diligently for the men, who, from native virtue and genuine love of their country and mankind, have *already* rejected, in the sight of America, the alluring temptations which ambition and opportunity have heretofore presented to them.

A third cautionary idea is, that we avoid the man who has evidenced a vindictive spirit in his past life. Rather let the President of the United States be the man, who, while he has stedfastly resisted his own and his country's foes, and pursued them till they sought for peace, at least by retiring, shewed no desposition to wound even an enemy, that had ceased to be injurious.

A fourth cautionary idea is, to avoid placing a son of rapine in the seat of dignity and power. Can we find a man, who, having spent the best of his days in the service of America, has, in every period of duty, despised all the secret temptations of opportunity, and declined even the proffered rewards of his grateful country—the man, who, while he was exhibiting this glorious example of disinterested concern for the cause in which he was engaged, used his virtuous influence only in favor of the companions of his dangers and his toils. If you can draw from his retirement such a character as this, you need not fear from him a misapplication of the pecuniary powers with which the constitution may invest him.

A fifth cautionary idea is, not to put into this seat a person of too narrow circumstances, especially if he is a man of expensive habits, and one who has been reduced to that situation by imprudent or ostentatious living. But though a certain clear property may be very proper, an overgrown estate is by no means desirable.

In the sixth place, we should take care to call to this office a man, who really loves the people, of a candid generous temper, and of an observing and reflecting turn of mind. For there can be no doubt that this, like every other human work, will prove, on experience, to have defects. Capacity and a turn for observation and reflection are therefore necessary, to mark the dangers to which liberty, property, and national safety and character may be exposed, by the unobserved doors which may appear to be left open to domestic and foreign enemies. Let us then fix on an able and tried friend to the people, who will honestly tell them of those opportunities of injuring them, which even his office may afford.

It may perhaps be said visionary by some, to expect in one individual a concurrence of circumstances and of virtues so favorable to the public happiness. But may it not be said with more propreity, that if the people of America do not see and feel that this blessing is within their reach, they do not deserve to possess it?

MODESTUS.

*—Pennsylvania Gazette*, 5 March 1788. Reprinted in the *New-York Morning Post*, 11 March, and the Boston *American Herald*, 20 March.

# "A Tissue of Virtues"

※ ※

FEDERAL ELECTIONEERING.

There is a man, in the United States, who must present himself to the consideration of every freeman thereof, as a candidate for the important station of PRESIDENT of the UNITED STATES. He is known

As disinterested—and therefore it is certain that he will not fleece us.

As having voluntarily laid down his former power—and therefore that he will not abuse those he may receive hereafter.

As having no son—and therefore not exposing us to the danger of an hereditary successor.

As being of a most amiable temper—and therefore that he will not be vindictive or persecuting.

His character, in short, is A TISSUE OF VIRTUES, and as there are some of our countrymen who doubt the safety of the proposed government, it is happy for us that we have such an approved and faithful citizen to employ in the experiment.

—*Massachusetts Centinel*, 26 March 1788. Reprinted in the *Pennsylvania Journal*, 9 April; *Maryland Journal*, 15 April; Baltimore *Maryland Gazette*, 15 April; *Virginia Independent Chronicle*, 23 April; and *Virginia Centinel*, 30 April.

# "I Wish He Had a Son"

✝ ✝

ANTHONY WAYNE TO MARQUIS DE LAFAYETTE,
SAVANNAH, 4 JULY 1788

I have just arrived from Phila: where I was obliged to attend in my place, as a member of the Pennsylvania Convention, & have the honor, & pleasure to Congratulate you upon the adoption of the Fœderal Constitution of America by *Nine* of the *States*, which secures its operation, from & after the first Monday in December next, & fixes this rising *Empire* upon so broad & solid a basis, as to insure her a conspicuous name, among the Nations; an *event*, that must afford the most pleasing sensation to a nobleman, who acted so principal a part upon her *theatre* & fought & bled in defence of her liberties, from her *coldest*, to her *hotest* sun; our Illustrious friend *Genl. Washington* will be her first—President (or by whatever other name the world may please to call him). I wish he had a *Son*—

Thus far for American politicks—

—Wayne Papers, Historical Society of Pennsylvania. Wayne, known as a daring and resourceful officer, attained the rank of brigadier general during the Revolution. As his last command during the war, his troops occupied Savannah. The Georgia legislature gratefully granted Wayne, originally from Pennsylvania, a large rice plantation.

# Endangered Laurels

※ ※

... We have, indeed, been told, a new order of things is to arise in our political hemisphere; but, I fear, it is more to be hoped for than expected. Already those who are fixed upon to fill its dignities, share the fate of their predecessors in abuse; who can say if they will equal them in success? Oh, Washington! I see thee quit thy Sabine fields, thy rural concerns, with fear, to immerge once more—not, indeed, into fields of military glory, but—into the thorn-covered path of political administration. None of thy votaries will wish thy patriotic ardor more success than I shall; but none is more afraid, that the laurels thou hast so deservedly acquired in war, may be at least assailed, if not obscured, in peace. The good and virtuous, I know, will oppose it; but their voice, alas! is but seldom heard, in the uproar of political dissention, and the war and virulence of contending factions. Yet, the country cannot do without thee; therefore *accept*; may Heaven, that sees, preserve and recompence thy disinterested virtue!

—Philadelphia *Federal Gazette*, 24 November 1788. Reprinted in the *Massachusetts Centinel*, 31 December.

# "The Key-Stone to
# Our Political Fabrick"

☙ ☙

ELIAS BOUDINOT TO GEORGE WASHINGTON,
NEW YORK, 6 APRIL 1789

I do most sincerely & affectionately congratulate my Country, on the unanimous election of your Excellency to the Presidency of the united States.

The importance of this transaction, is so great in my estimation that I consider it, under Providence, as the key-Stone to our political Fabrick. It is from this Consideration alone, that I can rejoyce with you Sir, as a private Friend, on your elevation to this dignified but difficult Office; by which you must again leave, all the sweets of domestic Felicity, which to yourself individually considered, cannot be repaid by all the honors of the world—I feel your delicate Situation—You have no choice in this great Business—Providence & your Country call, and there is no place for a refusal— The Sacrifice is required & the Offering must be made. . . .

—Washington Papers, Library of Congress. Boudinot, a wealthy Elizabeth Town, N.J., lawyer, had been President of Congress in 1782–83 and acting Secretary for Foreign Affairs from 1783 to 1784. He was elected a member of the first U.S. House of Representatives.

# "A Crisis that Requires a Washington!"

☙ ☙

ANTHONY WAYNE TO GEORGE WASHINGTON,
RICHMOND, GEORGIA, 6 APRIL 1789

Accept of my warmest & sincerest congratulations, upon your appointment to the *Presidency* of the United States of America! & altho' it cannot add to the Illustrious Character, you have so justly merited & established through the World, yet it reflects additional honor upon the *Western Empire*—by a display of her Wisdom—prudence & Gratitude, in the choice she has made of her greatest soldier—ablest statesman—& truest friend, to preside over her!

The task she has assigned you is ardious—but you are equal to it—the unbounded confidence placed in you, by every class of Citizens (which no other man cou'd expect or hope for) will contribute to render it less difficult—in fact—it is a Crisis that requires a Washington! I am therefore tempted to take the liberty, as an individual, sincerely devoted to you, & to my Country, to pray you to accept of the trust now committed to your charge! & at the same time to offer my ready & best services, shou'd they be at any time wanted, either in the Civil or Military line, in any quarter of America. . . .

—Henry E. Huntington Library, San Marino, California.

# Called by the Voice of America

♟ ♟

CHARLES THOMSON TO GEORGE WASHINGTON,
MOUNT VERNON, 14 APRIL 1789

The president of the Senate [John Langdon], chosen for the special occasion, having opened and counted the votes of the Electors in the presence of the Senate & the house of Representatives I am honored with the commands of the Senate to wait upon your Excellency with the information of your being elected to the office of President of the United States of America. This commission was entrusted to me on account of my having been long in the Confidence of the late Congress & charged with the duties of one of the principal civil departments of Government.

I have now Sir to inform you that the proofs you have given of your patriotism and of your readiness to sacrifice domestic ease and private enjoyments to preserve the liberty & promote the happiness of your Country, did not permit the two houses to harbour a doubt of your undertaking this great this important Office to which you are called not only by the unanimous votes of the Electors but by the voice of America. I have it therefore in command to accompany you to New York where the Senate & the house of Representatives of the United States are convened for the dispatch of public business.

In executing this part of my commission where personal gratification coincides with duty I shall wait your time & be wholly governed by your convenience.

—Washington Papers, Library of Congress. One of the leaders of the Philadelphia Sons of Liberty, Thomson had served as secretary of the Continental and Confederation Congresses from 1774 to 1789.

# Scarcely Left With an Alternative

♟ ♟

GEORGE WASHINGTON TO CHARLES THOMSON,
MOUNT VERNON, 14 APRIL 1789

I have been long accustomed to entertain so great a respect for the opinion of my fellow citizens, that the knowledge of their unanimous suffrages having been given in my favour scarcely leaves me the alternative for an Option. Whatever may have been my private feelings and sentiments, I believe I cannot give a greater evidence of my sensibility for the honor they have done me than by accepting the appointment.

I am so much affected by this fresh proof of my country's esteem and confidence, that silence can best explain my gratitude—While I realize the arduous nature of the task which is conferred on me and feel my inability to perform it, I wish there may not be reason for regreting the choice. All I can promise is only that which can be accomplished by an honest zeal.

Upon considering how long time some of the gentlemen of both houses of Congress have been at New York, how anxiously desirous they must be to proceed to business and how deeply the public mind appears to be impressed with the necessity of doing it immediately I cannot find myself at liberty to delay my Journey—I shall therefore be in readiness to set out the day after to morrow, and shall be happy in the pleasure of your company. For you will permit me to say that it was a peculiar gratification to have received the communication from you.

—Enclosed in Thomson's letter to the President of the Senate, 24 April 1789, RG 46, Records of the United States Senate, National Archives.

# Obeying the Country's Call

※ ※

GEORGE WASHINGTON TO JOHN LANGDON,
MOUNT VERNON, 14 APRIL 1789

I had the honor to receive your Official Communication, by the hand of Mr Secretary Thompson, about one o'clock this day. Having concluded to obey the important & flattering call of my Country, and having been impressed with an idea of the expediency of my being with Congress at as early a period as possible; I propose to commence my journey on thursday morning which will be the day after to morrow.

—Lilly Library, Indiana University.

# An "August Spectacle"

※ ※

This day His Excellency the PRESIDENT OF THE UNITED STATES arrived in this city, about one o'clock, accompanied by the President of the State, the Chief Justice, the Speaker of the Assembly, the Attorney General, the Honorable Mr. Read, and Secretary Thomson, the two city troops of horse, a body of light infantry, and a numerous concourse of citizens on horseback and foot.

HIS EXCELLENCY rode in front of the procession, on horseback, politely bowing to the spectators who filled the doors and windows, by which he passed. The bells were rung, and a feu de joye was fired as he moved down Market and Second-streets, to the City Tavern.

The joy of our whole city upon this august spectacle, cannot easily be described. Every countenance seemed to say, Long, long live GEORGE WASHINGTON, THE FATHER OF THE PEOPLE! At 3 o'Clock, his Excellency sat down to an elegant Entertainment at the City Tavern, prepared for him by the citizens of Philadelphia. His Excellency having travelled with great expedition from Mount Vernon, proposes to rest in our city, this afternoon, and to set off early to-morrow morning for New-York, where he will receive that power, which is infinitely preferable to a hereditary crown, inasmuch as it is conferred upon *merit*, by the unanimous and free suffrages of the Representatives of near three millions of affectionate and grateful People.

—Philadelphia *Federal Gazette*, 20 April 1789.

# "*The Hero at His Country's Call*"

X X

INSCRIBED
TO THE FATHER OF HIS COUNTRY.

While *greater bards* invoke a muse of fire,
And, borne on Fancy's wing, to Heaven aspire;
In strains majestic sing thy well-earn'd fame,
And to a wondring world thy worth proclaim;
Shall thy untutor'd muse, with feeble lays,
Attempt a subject which transcends *their* praise?
Yes, gen'rous chief, the grateful talk be mine,
While simple truth shall dictate ev'ry line,

To give a plain, a just, but concise view
Of Freedom's darling Son, great Sir—of *you*.——
    In Fancy's fields let tyrant's flatt'rers stray:
Wretches who make the human race their prey
Might shock mankind, if seen without disguise,
And bid their gen'rous indignation rise——
To sanction guild and varnish flagrant crimes,
Ignoble task! the fawning flatt'rer rhymes;
But rhymes in vain—Beneath the mask are seen,
Lurking, with haggard looks, and frightful mien,
Rapine and murder, avarice and pride,
With ev'ry vice the poet strives to hide.
Thus too th' abandon'd prostitute[1] presumes
With patches, paints; with washes, and perfumes,
To hide her loss of honor and of fame,
And strive, at least, *to form* a virtuous dame——
Unhappy female! all *her* wiles are vain;
The virtuous fair one, modest, neat, and plain,
(True tests of virtue!) needs no foreign art,
To warm, inspire, and captivate the heart:
For the chaste nymph, with secret pride, can boast
That she's, "when unadorn'd—adorn'd the most."[2]—
Let then the muse all arts of flatt'ry shun,
Nor once offend the ear of Washington
With durgid bombast or high sounding praise——
Come, Candor, come and pen these honest lays.
First see the hero at his country's call
Leaving his peaceful home, his friends, his all,
Rushing impetuous to the hostile field
And forcing Britain's chosen troops to yield.
What toils what hardships did he undergo!
What variegated scenes of human woe,
Thro' eight successive years, did he withstand,
To purchase freedom for his native land!

[1]Great Britain.
[2]Quoted from James Thomson's *Autumn* (line 204), which was
published in 1730.

With him the naked soldier could sustain
The winter's piercing frost, the snow and rain:
The gallant chief inspir'd each gen'rous soul
With freedom's sacred flame, and to the goal
Of glory led them on, 'till, peace procurred, ⎫
Freedom obtained, and happiness restor'd, ⎬
The gallant hero sheath'd the deathful sword— ⎭
That sword which ne'er was drawn but to oppose
Fair virtue's, freedom's, and his country's foes——
Then crown'd with laurels to his sabine farm
Return'd with joy. No more the dire alarm
Of dreadful war invites him to the field,
Columbia's rights from foreign force to shield.
But other foes too soon their place supply'd——
Licentiousness with faction at her side,
Detested fiends! had almost overthrown
That glorious Freedom by his prowess won.
'Tis thus while mariners Charybdis shun,
That they oft' times by Scylla are undone:[3]
Short-sighted mortals, ever prone to stray.
Seldom or never steer the middle way.
Lo now again th' illustrious Chief appears,
Relieves our sufferings, and dispels our fears,
Saves by his councils, what his arms have won,
And shows himself bright Freedom's fav'rite Son.
    Immortal worthy! long may'st thou preside
With honor o'er thy Country's peace, and guide
A grateful People to true happiness,
Oh may propitious Heaven thy measures bless!
May faction's cursed voice no more be heard;
May modest merit find its due reward;
May Science, parent of each useful art,

[3]In Greek mythology, Charybdis was the legendary gulf waters
that thrice daily rushed forward and then retreated creating a chasm
or whirlpool that unwary vessels could not escape. While mariners
eschewed Charybdis, they sometimes were surprised by the six-
headed monster snake Scylla, which would, if possible, seize a
mariner in each of its mouths.

Her chearing influence to our land impart—
Long may'st thou live, and when to Heaven
      remov'd,
Oh may thy worth, thy virtue be approv'd!—
May future ages still applaud thy fame,
And tyrants only shudder at thy name.

—Philadelphia *Federal Gazette*, 20 April 1789.

# *"A Second Time Called Upon"*

The fears of many honest, but scrupulous republicans, that the energy of the new government, might render it unfavorable to liberty, are at length subsided. All their apprehensions have been removed, by the election of their beloved WASHINGTON, to fill the office of first Magistrate of the United States. Under *his administration* they are convinced they have nought to fear; and they have too good an opinion of his patriotism, to suppose him capable of either forming, or sanctioning by his approbation, any system of government, which might have a tendency to destroy *at a future period*, that inestimable liberty, for which he bravely contended, till his generous efforts were crowned with merited success.

The *unanimous* vote of three millions of free Citizens, in favor of this distinguished Farmer, Hero and Statesman; and the unspeakable joy, with which he has been welcomed by all classes of people, on his way to New-York, are not only the greatest honors, that ever were conferred on man, but the happiest presages of the future greatness and respectability of our country.[1] In this city he met with the most grateful and kind reception, as well from those who were some time since violent in their opposition to the new government, as from its zealous friends and advocates. Some of the former description partook of the entertainment prepared for him, and chearfully concurred in the different patriotic and federal toasts, that were given on the occasion; while others, who had entertained like sentiments, were among those who presented written addresses to His Excellency, expressive of their esteem for his Person, and their best wishes for the happiness and prosperity of the United States, under his administration.

What a pleasing reflexion to every patriotic mind, thus to see our citizens again united, in their reliance on this great Man, who is a second time called upon, to be the Savior of his country! Who, possessing the full confidence of the People, is of all others the most likely to calm the turbulence of party spirit; and to unite all parties in the great duty which they owe their country, that of endeavoring, by their combined exertions, to raise her from that degraded rank, in the scale of nations, into which she has unhappily fallen; and speedily to advance her to that exalted station, to which she is justly entitled from her situation, soil, and vast resources; from her being the last retreat of Liberty and Justice; and from the asylum which is here opened for the injured and oppressed of all nations.

If many were thought warm in their opposition to the new constitution, let it be recollected, that we live under a democratical government; where, from the freedom of debate and enquiry that attends the discussion of political subjects, party bickerings are unavoidable.—Heat begets heat, and from the continual fer-

---

[1]This sentence was reprinted in the *Gazette of the United States*, 25–29 April 1789 ("The Only Reply," below).

ment, which is generally kept up, both parties are mutually irritated, and too often proceed to lengths, that their cooler judgment would disapprove. Candor must own, that, during the late contest, relative to the new constitution, the heat and violence of party were not confined to its opponents. But thanks to the enlightened reason and sound patriotism of the citizens of America, those temporary feuds are almost banished from amongst us.

The conduct of the opposers of the constitution, in thus concurring with the majority of their fellow citizens, it is to be hoped, is not altogether owing to General WASHINGTON's being appointed President; but has been considerably influenced by that truly republican spirit, which suggests the propriety of being ruled by a *majority*. Indeed, were it not for this, we should find every attempt to establish order and government, or to preserve liberty, vain and unsuccessful; and, having fallen a prey to the Dæmon of anarchy, we should be worse than beasts of prey—we should prey upon each other.

—Philadelphia *Federal Gazette*, 23 April 1789. Reprinted in the *New York Daily Gazette*, 30 April.

# "Sacred Freedom's Delegated Voice"

⚔ ⚔

An O D E,
*Most respectfully inscribed to his* EXCELLENCY GEN-
ERAL WASHINGTON, *on being chosen President of the
United States.*

## I.

Where fair Columbia spreads her wide domain
O'er many a lengthen'd hill, and sylvan plain,
In mystic vision wrapt, far to the south,
Array'd in all the bloom of rosy youth,
    A cherub form arose.
O'er the blue Heavens her showy pinions spread,
Celestial tints illum'd her starry head,
Bright as the radiant God of Day,
Soft as the fleecy cloud, or milky-way,
    Her shining vestment flows.
Her hand sustains the trump of fame,
Its blasts aloud her will proclaim;
    As high in air she hung,
O'er where Mount-Vernon's odours breathe,
She dropt immortal Glory's wreathe,
    Then, northward soaring, sung—
The music of the spheres resounding to her tongue.

## II.

Heaven-born Freedom, sent to save,
By actions, glorious as brave,
With every godlike virtue fraught,
Which either peace or war hath taught,
    Behold your Hero come!
Call'd by his country's urgent voice,

O'er her high councils to preside,
By ev'ry breast's united choice,
Call'd, the storm-beat helm to guide,
    He leaves his rural dome.
On all his steps see smiling Concord wait,
And harmony pervade each happy State—
See Public Confidence her arms expand,
While glad'ning gratulations echo o'er the land.

### III.

With soul at unambitious rest,
Yet glowing for the public weal;
Still must Columbia's dear bequest
O'er philosophic ease prevail.
    To hold with steady hand,
A free, a just restricting rein,
Wild jarring discord to restrain;
As government's revolving ear
Through placid peace, or horrid war,
    Obeys his mild command.
Thine be the bliss, great son of fame!
(As still hath been thine only aim)
To bid stern Justice poise her equal scale—
Reviving Commerce spread the swelling sail,
With golden prospects fraught, from ev'ry gale.

### IV.

Those laurel-trophies won through seas of blood,
Unequall'd in historic fame;
Those priceless labours for the public good
Had well immortaliz'd thy name,
    And claim'd a world's applause.
Now all the honours of the field,
All splendid conquest e'er could yield,
Combine with universal praise,
On high thy matchless worth to raise,
    The guardian of our laws.

Not rear'd by tumult in a giddy hour,
The crested idol of despotic power;
But sacred Freedom's delegated voice,
Thy grateful country's uncorrupted choice.

### V.

No Alexander's mad career,
No Cæsar's dictatorial reign,
No dazz'ling pomp that sceptres wear,
Thy soul with thirst of power could stain,
    A greater honour's thine.
Approving millions place in you
That power they would reflective view—
Diffusing all that's good and great
Through each department of the State:
    Thy bright'ning virtues shine,
With more effulgence round thy head,
With more essential honours spread,
Than sparkling toys that gild the tyrant's brow;
Worn but to court his cringing slaves to bow.

### VI.

As yon bright spheres that circling run,
With lucid splendour round the Sun,
    Diffuse their borrow'd blaze;
So may that senatorian band,
Assembled by a virtuous land,
    As on thy worth they gaze;
Reflect the light thy virtues yield,
The sword of justice bid thee wield,
    And anarchy erase.
The Federal Union closer bind,
    Firm public faith restore;
Drive discord from the canker'd mind,
    Each mutual blessing pour:
Then, when the glorious course is run,
Which Heav'n assign'd her WASHINGTON;

His soul let cherub-choirs convey
To all the triumphs of eternal day.

S. K.

*Bladensburg, April* 16, 1789.

—*Maryland Journal*, 24 April 1789. Reprinted in the *Virginia Centinel*, 13 May, and the *New Hampshire Spy*, 23 May.

# Beyond Raphael's Description

*Extract of a letter from a Gentleman in this city, to his Friend in the country, dated the 22d instant.*

"MY DEAR NEPHEW,

"I know you are anxious to hear the particulars of our late procession on the arrival of the President-General.—Being myself one of the *Dramatis Persona*, I shall give you a short detail of it, as well as my memory will serve.

"On the 18th instant, His Excellency THOMAS MIFFLIN, Esq. President of the State, the Honourable RICHARD PETERS, Esq. Speaker of our Legislature, and the old city Troop of Horse commanded by Colonel MILES,—proceeded as far as the line between this State and that of Delaware, under the pleasing expectation of meeting our beloved WASHINGTON, President-General of the United States: we were, however, disappointed, as he did not arrive at the line till early the next morning, when we were joined by another Troop from the city, commanded by Captain Bingham. After paying him the tribute of military honour due to his rank and exalted character, by proper salutes and otherwise, we escorted him into Chester, where we break-fasted, and rested perhaps a couple of hours.

"This great and worthy man, finding he could not possibly elude the parade which necessarily must attend manifestations of joy and affection, when displayed by a grateful people to their patriot benefactor, ordered his carriages into the rear of the whole line, and mounted an elegant horse, accompanied by the venerable patriot CHARLES THOMPSON, Esq. and his former Aid-de-Camp the celebrated Colonel HUMPHREYS; both of whom were also on horseback.

"On our way to the city, we were joined by de-tachments from the Chester and Philadelphia Troops of Horse, commanded by Captains M'DOWELL and THOMPSON, and also by a number of respectable citi-zens, at whose head was the citizen and soldier, his Excellency Arthur St. Clair, Esq. Governor of the western territory. Thus we proceeded to Mr. Grey's bridge, on Schuylkill; observing the strictest order and regularity during the march. But here my nephew, such a scene presented itself, that even the pencil of a Ra-phael could not delineate.

"The bridge was highly decorated with laurel and other evergreens, by Mr. GREY himself, the ingenious Mr. PEALE and others, and in such a style, as to display uncommon taste in these gentlemen.—At each end there were erected magnificent arches, composed of laurel, emblematical of the ancient triumphal arches, used by the Romans, and on each side of the bridge a laurel shrubbery, which seemed to challenge even nature her-self for simplicity, ease, and elegance.—And as our be-loved WASHINGTON passed the bridge, a lad, beau-tifully ornamented with sprigs of laurel, assisted by a certain machinary, let drop, above the Hero's head, un-perceived by him, a civic crown of laurel.—There was also a very elegant display of variegated flags on each side the bridge, as well as other places, which alternately caught the eye, and filled the spectator's soul with admiration and delight.—

"But who can describe the heartfelt gratulations of more than twenty thousand free citizens, who lined every fence, field and avenue between the bridge and city—The aged Sire, the venerable Matron, the blooming Virgin, and the ruddy Youth were all emulous in their plaudits—nay, the lisping Infant did not withhold its innocent smile of praise and approbation.[1]

"In short all classes and descriptions of citizens discovered (and they felt what they discovered) the most undisguised attachment, and unbounded zeal for their dear Chief, and I may add, under God, the Saviour of their country.—Not all the pomp of majesty, not even Imperial dignity itself, surrounded with its usual splendour and magnificence, could equal this interesting scene.

"On approaching near the city, our illustrious Chief was highly gratified with a further military display of infantry, commanded by Captain JAMES REES, and artillery command by Captain JEREMIAH FISHER, two active and able officers: and here I must not omit to give due praise to that worthy veteran Major FULLERTON, for his zeal, activity, and good conduct on this occasion.

"The corps joined in the procession, and thousands of freemen, whose hearts burned with patriotick fire, also fell into the ranks almost every square we marched, until the column swelled beyond credibility itself; and

---

[1] A 1786 American edition of the Comte de Mirabeau's *Reflection on the Observations on the Importance of the American Revolution* contained the following admonition on "Education": "Begin with the infant in his cradle: let the first word he lisps be the name of WASHINGTON." Mirabeau's passage was an epigram on the title page of Noah Webster's *An American Selection of Lessons in Reading and Speaking* (Philadelphia, 1787). A short paragraph in the *Massachusetts Centinel*, 10 November 1787, ends: "a French philosopher, speaking of our illustrious Fabius, enraptured bids us to '*Begin with the infant in the cradle: Let the first word he lisps be* WASHINGTON!' " By the end of December this paragraph was reprinted at least ten times between New Hampshire and Maryland.

having conducted the man of our hearts to the city Tavern, he was introduced to a very grand and plentiful banquet, which was prepared for him by the citizens. At dinner a number of patriotick toasts were drank. The pleasures and festivity of the day being over, they were succeeded by a handsome display of fire-works in the evening. Thus I have given you a faint idea of this glorious procession, and of the universal joy which inspired every heart upon this interesting, this important occasion.

I am dear Nephew, &c."

—*Gazette of the United States*, 25–29 April 1789.

# The Trenton Ladies' Sonata

⚔ ⚔

Yesterday morning [21 April] after receiving and answering several addresses, he set off for New-York. The city troops of light horse paraded at ten o'clock in order to accompany him to Trenton; but his Excellency being obliged, on account of the rain; to ride in his carriage, insisted upon declining the honor they intended him; for he could not, he said, think of travelling under cover, while they were exposed to the rain on horseback.

How different is power when derived from its only just source, viz. THE PEOPLE, from that which is derived from conquest, or hereditary succession!—The first magistrate of the nations of Europe assume the titles of Gods, and treat their subjects like an inferior race of animals. Our beloved magistrate delights to show, upon all occasions, that he is a man—and instead of assuming the pomp of master, acts as if he considered himself the FATHER—the FRIEND—and the SERV-ANT of the PEOPLE.

This afternoon we were honoured with the presence of His Excellency the President of the United States [Cyrus Griffin], on his way to Congress. A troop of Horse, commanded by Capt. CARLE, a company of Light Infantry, commanded by Capt. HANIOR, completely equipped in full uniform, with a large concourse of the gentlemen, and inhabitants of the town and neighbourhood, lined the bank of the Delaware to hail his arrival: As soon as he set foot on the Jersey shore; he was welcomed with three huzzas, which made the shores reecho the cheerful sounds; and being saluted by the Horse and Infantry, was escorted to town in the following Order.

A party of Horse.
The Light Infantry.
His EXCELLENCY, on horseback,
Attended by Mr. Secretary THOMPSON, and Col.
HUMPHREYS.
The Light Horse.
The Gentlemen of the town and neighbourhood,
on Horseback.

When the Procession arrived at the bridge, which lies south of the town, they were surprised with a scene, to which no description can do justice.

As *Trenton* had been made twice memorable during the war, once by the capture of the Hessians, and again by the repulse of the whole British army, in their attempt to cross this bridge, the Evening before the battle of *Princeton*, a design was formed by the ladies of this place, and carried into execution solely under their direction, to testify to his Excellency, by the celebration of these actions, the grateful sense they retained of the safety and protection afforded by him, to the daughters of New-Jersey.

A triumphal arch was raised on the bridge, 20 feet wide, supported by thirteen pillars. The center of the arch, from the ground, was about 20 feet. Each pillar was intwined with wreaths of evergreen. The arch, which extended about 12 feet along the bridge, was covered with laurel, and decorated on the inside with evergreens and flowers. On the front of the arch, or that side to which His Excellency approached, was the following Inscription, in large gilt letters:

"THE DEFENDER OF THE MOTHERS,
WILL BE THE PROTECTOR OF THE
DAUGHTERS,"

The upper and lower sides of this Inscription were ornamented with wreaths of evergreens, and artificial flowers, of all kinds, made for the purpose, beautifully interspersed. On the center of the arch, above the inscription, was a Dome, or Cupola, of flowers and evergreens, encircling the dates of those glorious actions, inscribed in large gilt letters. The summit of the Dome displayed a large *Sun-Flower*, which pointing to the Sun, was designed to express this sentiment or motto:

"TO YOU ALONE."

As emblematic of the unparralled unanimity of sentiment, in the millions of the United States.

A numerous train of Ladies, leading their daughters in their hands, assembled at the arch, thus to thank their Defender and Protector.

Just as His Excellency passed under the arch, he was addressed in the following SONATA, composed and set to musick for the occasion, and sung by a number of young Misses, dressed in white, and crowned with wreaths and chaplets of flowers.

# SONATA.

Welcome, mighty Chief! once more,
Welcome to this grateful shore:
Now no mercenary foe
Aims again the fatal blow—
*Aims at thee the fatal blow.*

Virgins fair, and Matrons grave,
Those thy conquering arms did save,
Build for thee triumphal bowers.
Strew, ye fair, his way with flowers—
*Strew your Hero's way with flowers.*

Each of the Singers held a basket in their hands,
filled with flowers, which, when they sung,
"*Strew your Hero's way with flowers,*"
they scattered before him.

When His Excellency came opposite to the little
female Band, he honoured the ladies, by halting until
the Sonata was finished.

The Scene was truly grand; and the mingled sentiments which crowded into the mind, in these few
moments of solemn stillness, bathed many cheeks with
tears. The General most politely thanked the Ladies
for their attention, and the Procession moved on to his
lodgings.

The Ladies of Trenton have displayed a degree of
taste, elegance, and patriotism on this occasion, which
does them the highest honor, and I believe stands unex-
ampled; but what particularly merits observation, all
expense was most carefully avoided: The materials of
the structure were the most plain and unpolished, and
cost the Ladies but the labour of a few evenings in
preparing flowers.

The General being presented with a copy of the
*Sonata*, was pleased to address the following CARD to
the Ladies.

To the *Ladies* of Trenton, who were assembled on the 21st Day of April, 1789; at the Triumphal Arch, erected by them on the Bridge, which extends across the Assanpinck Creek.

### CARD.

*GENERAL WASHINGTON cannot leave this place, without expressing his Acknowledgments to the Matrons and Young Ladies, who received him in so novel and grateful a manner, at the triumphal Arch in Trenton, for the exquisite Sensations he experienced in that affecting moment.—The astonishing contrast between his former and actual situation at the same spot—the elegant Taste with which it was adorned for the present occasion—and the innocent appearance of the* white-robed Choir, *who met him with the gratalatory Song, have made such an impression on his remembrance, as, he assures them, will never be effaced.*
*Trenton, April 21, 1789.*

To Morrow he leaves this by sun rising.——May it rise to him, many, many years—and every year Hail him, like many past, THE FATHER OF HIS COUNTRY.

—*Gazette of the United States*, 25–29 April 1789. This account was reprinted throughout the country.

# *"Effusions of Gratitude"*

Thursday last [April 23], between 2 and 3 o'clock, P.M. the Most Illustrious PRESIDENT OF THE UNITED STATES arrived in this city [New York].

At *Elizabethtown*, he was received by a deputation of three SENATORS and five REPRESENTATIVES of the United States—and three OFFICERS of the STATE and

CORPORATION—with whom he embarked on board the Barge, built for the purpose of wafting him across the bay. Thirteen Pilots in white uniforms rowed this Barge—THOMAS RANDALL, Esq. acting as Cockswain.

It is impossible to do justice in an attempt to describe the Scene exhibited on his Excellency's approach to the city. Innumerable multitudes thronged the shores, the wharves, and the shipping—waiting with pleasing anticipation his arrival. His Catholick Majesty's[1] Sloop of War, the *Galviston*—the Ship *North Carolina*, (Mr. DOHRMAN's) and other vessels, were dressed, manned, and highly decorated. His Excellency's Barge was accompanied by several other Barges, in one of which, were the Hon. the Board of Treasury,—the Minister of Foreign Affairs [John Jay],—and the Secretary at War [Henry Knox]—besides a long train of vessels and boats from New-Jersey and New-York. As he passed the *Galviston* she fired a salute of 13 guns—The Ship *North Carolina*, and the *Battery*, also welcomed his approach with the same number.

The whole water scene was highly animated—moving in regular order—the grand Gala formed an object the most interesting imaginable.

On His Excellency's arrival at the Stairs, prepared and ornamented, at MURRAY's wharf, for his landing, he was saluted by Col. BAUMAN's artillery, and received and congratulated by his Excellency the Governour [George Clinton], and the Officers of the State and Corporation—from whence the PROCESSION moved, in the following Order, viz.

Colonel LEWIS,
Accompanied by Majors' MORTON and VAN HORNE.
Troop of Dragoons,
Capt. STAKES.
German Grenadiers,
Capt. SCRIBA.

[1]King Charles IV of Spain.

*Band of Musick.*
Infantry of the Brigade,
Captains' SWARTOUT and STEDDIFORD.
Grenadiers,
Capt. HARSIN.
Regiment of Artillery,
Colonel BAUMAN.
*Band of Musick.*
General MALCOLM, and AID.
Officers of the Militia—two and two.
Committee of Congress.
The PRESIDENT—Governour CLINTON.
President's Suite.
Officers of the State.
Mayor [James Duane] and Aldermen of New-York.
The Reverend Clergy.
Their Excellencies the French and Spanish Ambassa-
dours in their Carriages.
The whole followed by an immense concourse of
Citizens.

The Procession moved through *Queen Street* to the House prepared for the reception of the President—from whence He was conducted, without form, to the GOVERNOUR's, where his Excellency dined.

"This great occasion arrested the publick attention beyond all powers of description—the hand of industry was suspended—and the various pleasures of the capital were concentered to a single enjoyment"—All ranks and professions expressed their feelings, in loud acclamations, and with rapture hailed the arrival of the FATHER OF HIS COUNTRY.

The illumination of the city on Thursday evening was brilliant. The transparent paintings in various quarters did honour to the ingenuity and publick spirit of the parties concerned in their exhibition.

The Scene on Thursday last was sublimely great—beyond any descriptive powers of the pen to do justice to—How universal—and how laudable the curiosity—

How *sincere*—and how *expressive* the sentiments of respect and veneration!—All ranks appeared to feel the force of an expression, that was reiterated among the crowd—"WELL, HE DESERVES IT ALL!"

The spontaneous effusions of gratitude to the illustrious WASHINGTON, exhibited by all ranks of people, in a thousand various indications of the sublime principle, are the highest reward that virtue enjoys, next to a conscious approbation which always precedes such undissembled testimonials of publick affection.

Many persons who were in the crowd, on Thursday, were heard to say, that they should now die contented—nothing being wanted to complete their happiness, previous to this auspicious period, but the sight of the Saviour of his Country.

Some persons, advanced in years, who hardly expected to see the illustrious President of the States, till they should meet him in Heaven, were in the concourse on Thursday, and could hardly restrain their impatience, it being in a measure deprived of the high gratification, by the eagerness of the multitudes of children and young people, who probably might long enjoy the blessing.

It was a very lively mark of affection as well as an ingenious display of fancy, in the circumstance of ranging a lovely group of little girls on *Trenton Bridge*, to sing an Ode, composed for the occasion, while the beloved of all hearts was passing it, on his way to New-York.

A sloop that ran out of Elizabethtown, to join in the Gala, from that place, on Thursday, was filled with a collection of the fair Daughters of Columbia, who enlivened the scene by singing a variety of expressive and animated songs.

Merit must be great, when it can call forth the *voluntary* honours of a free and enlightened people: But the attentions shewn on this occasion, were not merely *honorary*, they were the tribute of gratitude, due to a man whose life has been one series of labours for the publick good—upon a scale of eminence, that Heaven never before assigned to a mortal. These labours have been atchieved so perfectly, that future ages shall acknowledge the justice of the poet, when they read,

"So near perfection, that he stood
"Upon the boundary line,
"Of finite, from infinite good,
"Of human from divine."

The wise, the good, and truly great, among mankind, have uniformly professed to be actuated by similar motives in their pursuits, either as *governed*, or *governours*, *patriots*, *heroes*, *statesmen*, *or legislators*—those motives have been the PUBLIC GOOD, under the Superintendence of DIVINE PROVIDENCE.— What can exhibit the dignity of human nature in greater perfection?

—*Gazette of the United States*, 22–25 April 1789.

# *"Hail, Thou Auspicious Day!"*

罢 罢

ODE
*Sung on the arrival of the*
PRESIDENT *of the* UNITED STATES.
Tune *"God save &c."*.
(*Composed by Mr. L—.*)

HAIL, thou auspicious day!
Far let America
  Thy praise resound;
Joy to our native land!
Let ev'ry heart expand,
For Washington's at hand.
  With glory crown'd!

Thrice blest Columbians hail!
Behold, before the gale,
    Your CHIEF advance;
The matchless HERO's nigh!
Applaud HIM to the sky,
Who gave you liberty,
    With gen'rous France.


Illustrious Warrior hail!
Oft' did thy sword prevail
    O'er hosts of foes;
Come and fresh laurels claim,
Still dearer make thy name,
Long as immortal Fame
    Her trumpet blows!


Thrice welcome to this shore,
Our leader now no more,
    But ruler thou;
Oh truly good and great!
Long live to glad our state,
Where countless honors wait
    To deck thy brow.


Far be the din of arms,
Henceforth the olive's charms
    Shall war preclude;
These shores a HEAD shall own,
Unsully'd by a throne,
Our much lov'd WASHINGTON,
    The great, the good.


—*Gazette of the United States*, 22–25 April 1789. Within a
month, this poem was reprinted in nineteen newspapers
throughout the United States and as a broadside in New
York.

# "The Only Reply"

⚔ ⚔

We have heard much of the BIRTH DAY of our COLUMBIA: Her natal hour is dated on the 19th of APRIL, 1775[1].

TO MORROW is the Day of her ESPOUSALS— when, in presence of the KING of KINGS, the solemn Compact will be ratified between her, and the darling object of her choice.

May the date from that moment, the brightest Scenes of Freedom and Happiness, under the auspices of the wise and glorious Administration of the PRESIDENT OF HER AFFECTIONS.

In the evening the FIRE WORKS, prepared under the direction of the ingenious Col. BAUMAN, will irradiate the Hemisphere, which, in conjunction with well-fancied Illuminations, in various parts of the city, will conclude the Scene with a splendid exhibition.

\* \*

It is undoubtedly a new and astonishing thing under the sun, that the UNIVERSAL SUFFRAGES OF A GREAT AND VARIOUS PEOPLE, SHOULD CENTRE IN ONE AND THE SAME MAN; for it is evidently a fact, that was every individual *personally* consulted as to the man whom they would elect to fill the office of PRESIDENT of this rising empire, the only reply from *New-Hampshire* to *Georgia* would be *WASHINGTON,*

The *unanimous* vote of three millions of free citizens, in favour of this distinguished Farmer, Hero, and Statesman; and the unspeakable joy, with which he has been welcomed by all classes of people, on his way to New-York, are not only the greatest honours, that ever

[1]The date of the battle of Lexington.

were conferred on man, but the happiest presages of the future greatness and respectability of our country.[1]

America has discovered a superiority of genius in her sons, by a great variety of striking instances:—The whole course of the late glorious revolution, testifies to the truth of this observation: The adoption of the new constitution confirms it in an eminent degree: It remains for her to complete the splendour of her character, by giving a successful operation to the new government. Wisdom may devise—experience and patriotism may enforce her dictates, but the great body of the people must give the *tone* to the administration of the new system——*And they will do it.*

—*Gazette of the United States,* 25–29 APRIL 1789.

[1]This paragraph was first printed in the Philadelphia *Federal Gazette,* 23 April ("A Second Time Called Upon," above).

# *Nature Takes a Turn*

꽃 꽃

TO THE PRESIDENT OF THE UNITED STATES.
  Oft times, when rapture swells the heart,
  Expressive silence can impart
     More full the joy sublime:
  Thus WASHINGTON, my wond'ring mind,
  In every grateful ardor join'd,
     Tho' words were out of time.

  The muse of ******'s peaceful shade,
  Gave way to all the gay parade
     For transport of her own;

She felt the tear of pleasure flow,
And gratitude's delightful glow
    Was to her bosom known.

Triumphal arches—gratulating song,
And shouts of welcome from the mixed throng,
    Thy laurels cannot raise.
We praise ourselves; exalt our name
And in the scroll of time, we claim
    An int'rest in thy bays.

But 'erst on Hudson's whit'ned plain,
Where the blue mists enshroud the slain,
    And Hero's spirits came;
    Anxious to seal thy future fate,
Each on his cloud, in awful state,
Pronounc'd thee good as well as great,
    And fill'd thy cup of fame.

While we the favorites of Heaven,
To whom these western climes are given,
    And halcyon days await,
May bless ourselves, and bless our race,
That God by his peculiar grace
    Chose thee to rule the state.

Fame as she flies, her trump shall sound,
To all the admiring nations round,
    And millions yet unborn
Will read the history of this day,
And as they read will pause—and say
    Here nature took a turn.

For in the annals of mankind,
Who ever saw a compact bind
    And empire's utmost bound;
Who ever saw ambition stand,

Without the power to raise her hand;
    While *one* the people crown'd.

New-Jersey, May 1789.

—New York *Daily Advertiser*, 8 May 1789. Reprinted in
the *Gazette of the United States*, 9 May; the Philadelphia
*Federal Gazette*, 15 May; and the *New Hapshire Spy*, 30
May.

# "*Our Fabian Queen*"

### ✠ ✠

## ON THE AMIABLE CONSORT OF OUR IL-LUSTRIOUS WASHINGTON'S PASSING THROUGH PHILADELPHIA, ON HER WAY TO NEW-YORK.

Touch, touch the string of rapt'rous joy!
    My fair one's eyes I've seen:
With rapture I the time employ
    To hail our *Fabian* Queen!

Pure, unaffected, and sedate,
    Surpass all pedigree;
What, tho' she fills no chair of state?
    She reigns still with the free.—

Meekness adorns her as a robe
    Of most transcendent die!
With goodness join'd, o'er all the globe
    The sister virtues fly!

Let Princes boast of titles great,
    Obtain'd by force or fraud!

Mere trappings of a pageant state!
And slaves their titles *laud!*
COLUMBUS.

—Philadelphia *Independent Gazetteer*, 25 May 1789. Reprinted in the Baltimore *Maryland Gazette*, 2 June, and the Richmond *Virginia Gazette*, 11 June. Martha Washington left Mount Vernon for New York on 16 May.

# Filling the Chair of State

### An ODE
### For INDEPENDENCE, July 4*th*, 1789.
### *By DANIEL GEORGE.*

'Tis done!—the edict past, by Heav'n decreed,
And *Hancock's* name confirms the glorious deed.
On this auspicious morn
Was *INDEPENDENCE* born:
Propitious day!
Hail! the United States! of blest America!
CHORUS.
*Fly, swift-wing'd Fame,*
*The news proclaim:*
*From shore to shore,*
*Let cannons roar;*
*And joyful voices shout* COLUMBIA'*s name.*


See haughty Britain, sending hosts of foes,
With vengeance arm'd, our freedom to oppose;
But *WASHINGTON the Great,*
Dispell'd impending fate,
And spurn'd each plan:
Americans, combine to hail the god-like man!

131

CHORUS.
*Fly, swift-wing'd Fame, &c.*

Let *Saratoga's* crimson plains declare
The deeds of GATES, that "thunderbolt of war:"
His trophies grac'd the field:
He made whole armies yield—
A vet'ran band:
In vain did *Burgoyne* strive his valor to withstand.[1]
CHORUS.
*Fly, swift-wing'd Fame, &c.*

Now *York-Town's* heights attract our wond'ring eyes,
Where loud artill'ry rends the lofty skies:
There *WASHINGTON* commands,
With *Gallia's* chosen bands,
A war-like train;
Like Homer's conquering Gods, they thunder o'er
the plain.
CHORUS.
*Fly, swift-wing'd Fame, &c.*

Pale terror marches on, with solemn stride;
*Cornwallis* trembles, Britain's boasted pride:
He, and his armed hosts,
Surrender all their posts
To *WASHINGTON*,
The friend of Liberty—*Columbia's* favourite son.
CHORUS.
*Fly, swift-wing'd Fame, &c.*

Now from *Mount Vernon's* peaceful shades again
The Hero comes, with thousands in his train:

[1]This stanza refers to the American victory of General Horatio
Gates over British General John Burgoyne at Saratoga, New York,
in October 1777.

132

'Tis *WASHINGTON the Great*
Must fill the chair of state,
Columbia cries;
Each tongue the glorious name re-echoes to the skies.

CHORUS.

*Fly, swift-wing'd Fame, &c.*

Now shall the useful arts of Peace prevail,
And Commerce flourish, favor'd by each gale;
Discord, forever cease!
Let Liberty, and Peace
And Justice reign;
For WASHINGTON protects the scientific train.

CHORUS.

*Fly, swift-wing'd Fame, &c.*

*Portland, (Massachusetts) June,* 1789.

—*Gazette of the United States*, 1 July 1789. Reprinted in the *Massachusetts Centinel*, 8 July; Portland, Maine, *Cumberland Gazette*, 10 July; *New Hampshire Spy*, 11 July; Richmond *Virginia Gazette*, 16 July; and *New York Journal*, 16 July. The July 1789 issue of the *Massachusetts Magazine* printed the sheet music.

# *Never to be Outshone*

🌣 🌣

*The two following ODES, (wrote for the occasion) were sung on Saturday last, by the gentlemen assembled at the Globe Tavern, to celebrate that glorious æra—*AMERICAN INDEPENDENCE.

## ODE FIRST.
### *To the Tune of* "God save the King."

"Hark! hark! the Hero comes!"
　Proclaim'd by shouts and drums,
　　And trump of Fame,
　Bellona's[1] favourite son.
　The illustrious WASHINGTON,
　Who glorious deeds has done,
　　God bless his name.

Thus shall his feats be sung,
(While envy bites her tongue)
　　To hear the lays:
Around this spacious frame,
Eccho shall spread the flame,
And thro' the world proclaim,
　　Great GEORGE's praise.

In Senate or the field,
Patriots and Warriors yield,
　　Nations admire;
In him the Graces beam,
In Virtue's walk, supreme,
Of every tongue the theme,
　　And breathing lyre.

[1] A Roman goddess of war.

134

Tho' Britain still can boast
Renowned Heroes lost,
　　Her *George* revere;
A *George* may heir her throne,
But *here*, a GEORGE alone,
Can never be outshone,
　　COLUMBIA'S HEIR.

*Heir* to command and sway,
The glories of our day,
　　By *right divine**:
*Heir* to our nation's love,
And blessings from above,
Thou Son of mighty Jove,[2]
　　Our *hearts* are thine.

　* The Vox Populi, *in the unanimous choice of
President WASHINGTON, has been as truly displayed,
as on any event whatever, and nothing but a pure
effort of divine Providence, could have produced such a
union of sentiment.*

ODE SECOND.
*To the same Tune.*

God save Columbia's son!
Long live great WASHINGTON!
　　Crown him with bays!
Shout, shout, America!
Wide over earth and sea,
Shout, in full harmony,
　　WASHINGTON's praise!

When Britain took the field,
Then his strong arm repell'd,
　　Fought and subdu'd!

[2]Jove, or Jupiter, was the father of the gods.

135

Now all victorious!
Mighty, and glorious!
He presides over us!
    Great, just and good!

Raise then to heav'n the song,
Pour in full tides along
    GRATITUDE's strains:
Say thou'rt our strength and stay!
Still we'll confess they sway,
Whilst o'er America
    WASHINGTON reigns!

—*New Hampshire Spy*, 7 July 1789. The first ode was reprinted in the *Massachusetts Centinel*, 15 July; *Gazette of the United States*, 18 July; Lansingburgh, New York, *Federal Herald*, 3 August; and York *Pennsylvania Herald*, 19 August.

# "Our Saviour and Our Guide"

🏴 🏴

G  *eneral!* immortaliz'd by virtuous fame!
E  *ngland's* brave foe! to *France* how dear thy name!
O  'er our young Senate hasten to preside;
R  ule a glad land; our Saviour and our Guide.
G  overn by law; and shew admiring men
(E  nvy may howl) OUR noblest citizen.

W  ise, valiant! may thy name still brighter grow;
A  nd make mankind to worth and virtue bow;
S  teady in justice to thyself and friends;
H  appy that people, which thy worth commends.
I  nstruction shall descend from sires to sons;
N  o name so great, so dear, as *Washington's.*
G  enerous and just! we dread from thee no wrong;
T  hy gallant deeds have silenc'd Envy's tongue.
O  ! to the warrior's add the statesman's praise,
N  or scorn once more a drooping land to raise.

### Additional Lines.
A bard, beyond the mountains, with firm toil,
Who near *Ohio* cultivates his soil,
Sends thee those verses, which thy deeds relate;
How small his talents! but the theme how great!
Unfavor'd by the nine[1] his youth he past;
These his first rhymes, and these perhaps his last.
Hear the glad wish, which animates *this* line;
*Be thou the people's shield!—and virtue thine!*

> —Philadelphia *Federal Gazette*, 20 August 1789. This poem
> was first printed in French in the *Federal Gazette* on 24
> April 1789. The editor requested "some ingenious
> correspondent to favor him with a translation," which a
> gentleman from Philadelphia supplied.

[1]The nine goddesses who presided over literature and the arts
and sciences.

# "Great Architect"

芝 芝

*An* ACROSTIC.

G reat patron of our noble art divine,
E xtend thy all enliv'ning orient ray,
O n Masonry with ardent lustre shine,
R efulgent shine—and usher in new day;
G reat architect, bright morning star of fame,
E ach Mason glories in his patrons name.

W hat's great and good, and beautiful to see,
A re all compriz'd, and to be found in thee;
S tatesman, hero, patriot, brother dear,
H umane, benevolent, just and sincere;
I ntrepid soldier, guardian of our land,
N e'er let us fall beneath oppressor's hand,
G ently lead and guide us on to fame,
T hat we may stand recorded with thy name;
O n Mason's hearts thy name shall stand secure,
N or be forgot while Masonry endures.

—*New York Weekly Museum*, 12 September 1789.

# "Phoenix of the Age"

### An Acrostick

G reat Hero! whose illustrious actions claim
E ternal blessings and an endless fame—
O f every virtue and each gift possest
R eligion reigns triumphant in his breast.
G rant him, almighty God! thy aid and health
E ver to rule these states and guard their wealth.

W hat power of Language can enough extoll
A Son of Liberty and friend to all—
S aviour and patron of Columbia!
H er sons revere thee and exult this day—
I n thee, their Favourite and firm support—
N ations applaud thee and thy friendship court.
G enerous deliverer of thy Country's right!
T hou hast prov'd victor over lawless might.
O f all the Conquerors in the historic page,
N one have surpass'd this Phœnix of the age.

—*Boston Gazette*, 14 September 1789. Reprinted in the *New Hampshire Recorder*, 1 October.

# "Great Without Pomp"

✠ ✠

(We have frequently noticed the tributes paid to our illustrious President by the Tuneful Bards of this country: The following will shew what has been said in England

OF GEN. WASHINGTON.)

Great without pomp, without ambition brave,
Proud, not to conquer fellow-men, but save;
Friend to the weak, a foe to none, but those
Who plan their greatness on their brethren's woes;
Aw'd by no titles—undefil'd by lust—
Free without faction, obstinately just;
Too wise to learn from *Machiavel's* false school,
That truth and perfidy by turns should rule;
Warm'd by *Religion's* sacred genuine ray,
That points to future bliss th' unerring way;
Yet ne'er controul'd by Superstition's laws,
That worst of tyrants in the noblest cause.

—*New Hampshire Gazette*, 18 November 1789. Reprinted in the *New Hampshire Spy*, 27 November; Hartford *American Mercury*, 30 November; Charleston, S.C., *City Gazette*, 3 December; *New York Daily Gazette*, 28 December; *Albany Gazette*, 13 September 1790; and the appendix to the Philadelphia *American Museum* for 1790.

# "An Angel in the Shape of Man"

✠ ✠

## POEM; On THE PRESIDENT
### of the UNITED STATES.

The Painter's pencil, and the Poet's lays,
Have paid the plaudit due to virtuous praise,

Impatient of her Sister Arts, so long,
Now Musick tunes the gratulary song.

    While grateful hearts with shouts of loud
        applause,
Hail the DEFENDER of his country's cause,
The CHIEF delighted, hears the loud acclaim,
For none, unheeding, hear the voice of FAME:
And feels, unlike the heroes of mankind,
The conscious plaudit of th' approving mind.
For pride may boast, yet merit only knows,
The inward bliss which worth alone bestows.
'Tis not the sick'ning blast of *party rage*,
Nor the envenom'd sting of *Slander's* page
Nor loathsome *Envy's* pestilential breath,
Can taint his laurels, with the blast of death.
Still uncorroded by the rust of years,
His name shall live commensurate with the spheres.
So the tall rock, high on the mountain's brow,
Securely stands, nor fears the storms below,
And while the winds the face of earth deform,
Laughs at the whirlwind, and derides the storm.

    Superiour beings wonder, when they find,
Such full perfection of a mortal mind;
That Heav'n should deviate from the accustom'd plan,
And form an Angel in the shape of Man.

When we assume the sober garb of age,
Our youth shall emulate the godlike rage,
And fondly listen to the historick song,
Nor think, for once, an old man's tale too long.
Then shall new *Homers* sing the CHIEFTAIN's
        wars,
And not a Woman's,[1] but a Nation's cause;

[1]Helen of Troy, whose abduction by Paris brought about the
Trojan War.

141

Nor need th' assistance of the bright abodes,
*Columbia's* Heroes supersede *his Gods.*
Then be the magick powers of Musick given,
To chant alternate, WASHINGTON and HEAV'N.

Musick can sway the passions at controul,
And now *deject*, and now *delight* the soul.
Smooth as the stream serenely flows along,
With all the fascinating charms of song.
Or if warm transports prompt the tear to flow,
Melt with the plaintive eloquence of woe,
Or flush the cheek with hope, and *blanch* with fear,
And from soft Pity steal th' *unconscious tear.*
But if too sanguine, in her favourite cause,
She *'tempts* the grateful tribute of applause,
She seeks, to justly praise the CHIEF divine,
Th' united efforts of the tuneful Nine!
*Cambridge, Dec.* 4, 1789.

—*Massachusetts Centinel*, 5 December 1789. Reprinted in the New York *Daily Advertiser*, 15 December, and the *Gazette of the United States*, 16 December.

# *"The Good and Great"*

*VERSES*, on GEORGE WASHINGTON, ESQUIRE,
The illustrious PRESIDENT of the UNITED STATES.

Call'd from the bosom of his calm retreat,
At once the Hero's and the Sage's seat;
See WASHINGTON! assumes the helm of state,
And watches kindly for *Columbia's* fate.
Not only great in war, alike in peace,
He lulls our fears and makes all discord cease;

Aw'd by his virtues, enemies admire,
And wish to emulate his noble fire.
Hail, happy Man, crown'd with immortal bays,
Before whose glory, sink the dwindled rays
Of royal pageantry! whilst ev'ry voice,
Hail thee their leader! and their only choice!
Long may this happy land enjoy thy name,
And distant nations spread thy rising fame;
While freedom's sons presided o'er by thee,
Shall rise in arms and arts, and *still be free*.
Pleas'd with the Guardian of their country's cause,
Confederated States shall shout applause;
On each *new Year* our triumphs we'll repeat,
And sing of WASHINGTON, the *good* and *great!*

—Broadside for the Baltimore *Maryland Gazette*, 1 January 1790.

# "Next unto the Trinity"

On the PRESIDENT of the United States.

Behold the matchless Washington—
His glory hath eclips'd the sun;
The lustre of his rays so bright,
'Tis always day, there's no more night.

The greatest sage upon the globe,
Well may he wear the imperial robe;
The greatest statesman in the realm,
Which fits him for to set at helm.

The brilliant crown upon his head,
The Patriot's friend and Tyrant's dread;
Long, long may he the crown possess,
And sway in sceptred rightiousness.

And when he drops this earthly crown,
He's one in Heav's of high renown;
He's deify'd, exalt him high,
He's next unto the Trinity.

My language fails to tell his worth,
Unless in Heav'n he is the fourth;—
This tribute due to Washington,
Revere him every mother's son.

—Keene *New Hampshire Recorder*, 9 September 1790.

# IV

※ ※

# MEETING
# THE PEOPLE

## *The Presidential Tours*

O NE OF GEORGE WASHINGTON'S "first determinations" when he became President was to
visit every state in the Union during his tenure in office.
Illness made an early trip impossible, but by the fall of
1789, the convalescing President was eager to begin his
travels. Such a journey, taken during Congress' recess,
would invigorate the President and give him "knowledge of the Country, the growth and Agriculture thereof
and the temper and disposition of the Inhabitants
towards the new government." Washington decided
first to travel throughout the Northern States that had
ratified the Constitution—New York, Connecticut,
Massachusetts, and New Hampshire.

The Northern, or as Washington called it, the Eastern tour, began on 15 October as the President was
escorted "some distance out" of New York City by
Chief Justice John Jay and Secretaries Alexander Hamilton and Henry Knox. It ended six weeks later when
the President arrived back home on 13 November.
Throughout the journey, Washington made regular entries in his diary detailing the events of the day as well
as his impressions of the country and people.

The President travelled with remarkable infor-
mality. He was accompanied by his two personal sec-

retaries—Tobias Lear and William Jackson—and six servants. Most of the time on the long stretches between towns, the President rode in a coach pulled by four horses with a postilion; but, just before entering a town, Washington often left the carriage and mounted his familiar white horse.

Inundated with invitations to be a house guest, Washington stayed only at public inns or taverns. This inconvenienced no private families, allowed for greater flexibility in scheduling, and avoided giving umbrage to those whose invitations were rejected.

The presidential party would usually start its daily journey between 6:00 and 7:00 each morning. After travelling ten to fifteen miles the entourage would stop for breakfast. After another hour or two on the road, the horses would be fed, and then the final leg of the journey would end in one of the many towns along the President's route. Each day the President passed through several small towns where the roads were "lined with citizens to hail him welcome." Often Washington was met on the outskirts of the larger towns and escorted in by militia, light-horse cavalry, or the leading citizens while church bells pealed and artillery saluted. To maintain orderliness in these larger towns, processions of the inhabitants (arranged by occupation, political office, or military rank) marched by the President in review. Congratulatory addresses, odes, and music were presented and the President responded. Public dinners were held at which the mandatory thirteen toasts were offered usually punctuated by one or thirteen cannon salutes after each toast. Occasionally the evening ended with a ball, where the President danced with many of the elegantly dressed ladies, who often wore "Washington sashes" emblazoned with an American eagle and the initials "G.W." Buildings were illuminated and fireworks lit the night-time sky. The next morning the presidential cavalcade started off again. (In some of the larger towns, such as New Haven, Hartford, Boston and Portsmouth, the President stayed for several days). But since travelling on the Sabbath was illegal in some New England states, and frowned upon in all of them, the presidential party did not travel on Sundays. The President, therefore, attended church services twice each Sunday, once in the morning and again in the afternoon.

In addition to his public ceremonies, Washington found time to do things he really enjoyed. He attended concerts, inspected a 74-gun French man-of-war, fished for cod off Portsmouth, talked with farmers along the way about their crops, and visited Revolutionary War battle sites, internal improvement projects and manufactories. Much to his dislike, he sat for a portrait in Portsmouth.

The most significant embarrassment on the Eastern tour occurred in Boston as Governor John Hancock conspicuously boycotted all of the celebrations honoring the President. Suffering from one of his many politically opportune attacks of the gout, the Governor sent word to Washington on Saturday evening that he was ill and that he wanted the President to come to the executive mansion. Washington explicitly informed the messengers (Lt. Governor Samuel Adams and two members of the Council) that he would not see the Governor "unless it was at my own lodgings." On Sunday Washington received a card from Hancock dated 12:30 stating, that, if the President was "at home and at leisure," the Governor would pay him a visit "in half an hour." He explained that he had not done so previously because he lay near death, but that he would "now hazard every thing as it respects his health" for a visit with the President. Washington responded with a card dated 1:00 P.M. in which he wrote that he was free until 2:00, but that the Governor should "not hazard his health on the occasion." Hancock quickly made the humbling journey and was carried into the President's quarters on a litter. Washington returned the visit the next day.

In late May 1790 Rhode Island ratified the Constitution. On 15 August, Washington embarked on the packet *Hancock* for Newport. He was accompanied by Secretary of State Thomas Jefferson, Governor of New York George Clinton, Supreme Court Justice John Blair, Rhode Island Senator Theodore Foster, South Carolina Representative William Loughton Smith, David Humphreys, and secretaries William Jackson and Thomas Nelson. The party arrived on 17 August and addresses were delivered to Washington to which he responded. Similar ceremonies occurred in Providence during the next two days. On the 19th, Washington left on the *Hancock* and arrived in New York City on 22 August.

A month after the Eastern tour ended, Governor Charles Pinckney of South Carolina invited the President to visit the South. "Not being master of my own time," Washington responded, he could make no promises, but he told Pinckney "that nothing would give me greater pleasure than to have it in my power to visit all the Southern States." Such a trip was at first planned for the fall of 1790 and then for the following spring. Anticipating the presidential visit, Southerners encouraged their communities to spruce up, repair or build new boats at ferries, and, in effect, outdo their Northern brethren in welcoming the President. Washington hoped that he could leave Philadelphia by mid-March 1791 in order to avoid being in the southernmost states after May. His close friend Henry Lee reminded him of "the pestilential effects of the southern sun in the hot season," hoping that Washington could be back home at Mount Vernon by the end of May.

Before leaving Philadelphia, Washington carefully prepared a detailed itinerary listing dates, places, and miles between towns. He obtained "the most accurate account . . . of the places and roads . . . and the distances between the former." He estimated the total length of the journey at 1,816 miles. The schedule would be demanding for the nearly sixty-year-old President and more so for the horses.

Washington began his Southern tour on Monday, 21 March as he left Philadelphia accompanied by his secretary William Jackson and five servants—a valet, two footmen, a coachman, and a postilion. They travelled with a chariot pulled by four horses, a light baggage wagon with two horses, and five saddle horses, one of which was Washington's old white stallion. The President wrote his secretaries of State, Treasury, and War that if any serious matter arose, they should consult with each other—and with Vice President John Adams, if he had not gone home to Massachusetts. If they believed that the President was needed, he would "return immediately"; otherwise, they should run the government in his absence.

The trip began with a near disaster. In order to avoid the bad roads between Delaware and Maryland, Washington decided to ferry his entourage from Rock Hall, Delaware, to Annapolis. During a violent nighttime storm, the inexperienced—or incompetent—captain grounded his ship twice at the mouth of the Severn River leading to Annapolis. After strenuous effort, the vessel was freed from the first grounding, but could not escape the second. The crew and passengers stayed awake the entire night, not knowing whether the ship would founder. As morning came, a boat from Annapolis rescued the President.

Washington spent a week at Mount Vernon catching up on business before the major portion of the Southern tour began. On 7 April he resumed his journey. A second accident occurred within a few miles of Mount Vernon as the party ferried across Ocquoquam Creek (about 100 yards wide) at Colchester. One of the chariot's lead horses, harnessed and hitched, frighted and fell overboard in the middle of the creek. With great difficulty, the horse was freed, but the disturbance so frightened the other three horses, that one after another in rapid succession they too jumped overboard. Miraculously, Washington reported, all the horses, the chariot, and the harnesses were saved without injury. From this point, no further accidents occurred.

The Southern tour proceeded much as its Northern counterpart. The party usually travelled between 35 and 45 miles a day with seldom a day off. At first the presidential party began its day's journey at 6:00 A.M. That soon changed to a 5:00 A.M. start and then an incredible 4:00 A.M. beginning during most of the last three weeks before the return to Mount Vernon on 12 June. Washington arrived home about a week earlier than expected, where he rested and caught up on business until departing northward on 27 June. He arrived in Philadelphia on Wednesday, 6 July.

Washington was pleased with his presidential tours. In a letter to Governor Alexander Martin of North Carolina, he said that his purpose in visiting the states "was not to be received with parade and an ostentatious display of opulence. It was for a nobler purpose. To see with my own eyes the situation of the Country, and to learn on the spot the condition and disposition of our Citizens. In these respects I have been highly gratified, and to a sensible mind the effusions of affection and personal regard which were expressed on so many occasions is no less grateful, than the marks of respect shewn to my official Character were pleasing in a public view." To his old friend David Humphreys he confided that "Each days experience of the government of the United States seems to confirm its establishment, and to render it more popular. A ready acquiescence in the laws made under it shews in a strong light the confidence which the people have in their representatives, and in the upright views of those who administer the government."

The presidential tours did much to unify the country behind President Washington and the new federal government. Opponents of the Constitution saw first-hand the tremendous support the people had for the new experiment. In a way, the tours marked the end of the Revolution. The *Gazette of the United States* reported that "The time to pull down, and destroy, is now past." It was now time "to build up, strengthen and support" the Constitution. The tours had demonstrated that these sentiments "pervade the minds of the people."

# Anticipating
# the Celebration

𝖤𝖤

*(The votaries of the Muses have favoured us with several ebulitions on the prospect of the arrival of the President of the United States in this metropolis. On such a subject, nothing but the sublime and beautiful, we think, ought to be admitted—But the following, flowing from the genuine feelings of gratitude and affection, though expressed in rather* outre *language, came too strongly recommended to be refused.)*

TO THE CITIZENS OF BOSTON.
The Man belov'd approaches nigh,
    Revere him, ye Bostonian sons,
Embrace the chance before you die,
    And canonade with all your guns.

Let lively squibs dance thro' the town,
    And pleasing rockets gild the air,
There's not a man can shew a frown,
    But all shall joyously appear.

Let punch in casks profusely flow,
    And wine luxuriantly be spread,
That townsmen all, both high and low,
    May hand in hand by mirth be led.
                       P.Q.

—*Massachusetts Centinel*, 21 October 1789.

# "The President's Young Servant"

CHARLES LEE COLES TO GEORGE WASHINGTON,
CHARLESTOWN, MASS., 22 October 1789

To the President of the United states

How Oft, Great Sir, has thy Sacred Name been Sounded in Our Infant Ears, By Our honrd. Father, and How Oft has our Tender Mother taught us to Love, Honour, and Obey, the Name of Washington, and, How Great should be Our gratitude to the supreme Ruler of the Universe, For preserveing us through our helpless Years, in war, to behold thy face in peace, and to Lisp forth, the Immortal praise, of the saviour of his Country.

I am in behalf of my Eight Brothers and Sisters, the Presidents Young Servant.

Charles Lee Coles. Aged 12 years.

—Washington Papers, Library of Congress. This letter was enclosed with another from John Coles, Charles' father, dated 27 October 1789, headed "The Poor Man's Prayer." In this letter, John Coles asked Washington to use his influence with Congress to enact a humane bankruptcy bill "Calculated to Defend the Helpless, honest, and industrious Man and to Grant him Time, to Labour for the Payment of his Just Debts and Seport of his Family. Which if thy Servant Miss Not, No Laws, within these States, Defend him in at Present." Many of the states at this time had severe bankruptcy laws that imprisoned debtors who could not meet their creditors' demands. The new Constitution gave Congress the power to pass uniform laws for bankruptcy.

FOR THE MASSACHUSETTS MAGAZINE.

## ODE TO COLUMBIA'S FAVOURITE SON.

Sung by the INDEPENDENT MUSICAL SOCIETY, on the arrival of THE PRESIDENT
at the TRIUMPHAL ARCH, in BOSTON, October 24, 1789.

SOLO.—*The Bass to this part to be sung very softly by one voice.*

Great Washington, the Hero's come, Each heart exulting hears the sound; See!

thousands their de-liv'- rer throng, And shout him wel - come all a - round.

### Chorus.
[To be sung briskly.]

Now in full chorus burst the song, And shout the deeds of Washington!

II.

There view Columbia's Favourite Son,
Her Father, Saviour, Friend and Guide !
There see th' Immortal WASHINGTON !
His Country's Glory, Boast and Pride !
*Now in full Chorus, &c.*

III.

When the impending storm of war,
Thick clouds and darkness hid our way,
Great WASHINGTON, our Polar Star,
Arose, and all was light as day !
*Now in full Chorus, &c.*

IV.

His bleeding country rous'd his soul,
Fair Freedom fir'd the Warriour's breast,
And drew the glitt'ring faulchion bold,
And round him clasp'd the martial vest.
*Now in full Chorus, &c.*

V.

Then nobly spake th' intrepid Chief,
" Freedom or Death be now my fate !
" This burnish'd blade no more I'll sheathe,
" 'Till Paris's made an Empire great !'';
*Now in full Chorus, &c.*

October, 178                I

From the *Massachusetts Magazine*, October 1789, p. 659.

# Columbia's Favourite Son

☰ ☰

On the President's arrival at the State-house, he ascended a temporary balcony, adjoining the gallery* where were a select Choir of Singers, who upon the President's appearance sang the following

ODE,
To Columbia's Favourite Son.

### I

GREAT WASHINGTON the Hero's come,
　　Each heart exulting hears the sound,
Thousands to their Deliverer throng,
　　And shout him welcome all around!
　　*Now in full chorus join the song,*
　　*And shout aloud great* WASHINGTON!

### II

There view *Columbia's* favourite Son,
　　Her Father, Saviour, Friend and Guide!
There see th' immortal WASHINGTON!
　　His Country's Glory, Boast and Pride!
　　*Now in full Chorus, &c.*

### III

When th' impending storm of War,
　　Thick clouds and darkness hid our way,
Great WASHINGTON our Polar Star
　　Arose; and all was light as day!
　　*Now in full Chorus, &c.*

*On the front of the gallery was printed in large letters, "TO THE MAN WHO UNITES ALL HEARTS." On the rear, "TO COLUMBIA'S FAVOURITE SON." And at the sides, "Boston relieved, 17th March, 1776."

## IV

'Twas on yon plains thy valour rose,
  And ran like fire from man to man:
'Twas here thou humbled *Paria's* foes,
  And chac'd whole legions to the main!
    *Now in full Chorus, &c.*

## V

Thro' countless dangers, toils and cares,
  Our Hero led us safely on—
With matchless skill directs the wars,
  Till Vict'ry cries—the day's his own!
    *Now in full Chorus, &c.*

## VI

His country sav'd, the contest o'er,
  Sweet peace restor'd his toils to crown,
The Warrior to his native shore
  Returns, and tills his fertile ground.
    *Now in full Chorus, &c.*

## VII

But soon Columbia call'd him forth
  Again to save her sinking fame,
To take the Helm, and by his worth,
  To make her an immortal name!
    *Now in full Chorus, &c.*

## VIII

Nor yet alone through *Paria's* shores,
  Her Fame her mighty trumpet blown;
E'n *Europe, Afric, Asia*, hears,
  And emulate the deeds he's done!
    *Now in full Chorus, &c.*

—*Boston Gazette*, 26 October 1789. By 19 November this
poem was reprinted twenty-two times. The music, with
four extra stanzas, was printed in the October issue of
the *Massachusetts Magazine*.

# "Glorious Father
of the Glorious Age"

Written on the arrival of the PRESIDENT into this
town.——(*Never before published.*)
Columbia's pride—the mighty chief draws nigh;
The boast of earth—and fav'rite of the sky!
Let ev'ry bard his tuneful numbers roll,
And fame's loud trump resound from pole to pole!

Ye peaceful swains, with shouts of gratitude,
Welcome the man, whose arm the foe subdu'd.
Ye sons of freedom, heroes, statesmen, join,
And round his brows the deathless wreath entwine.

Behold the empire's noblest son and shield,
Who led our hosts triumphant from the field,
Reduc'd proud warriors, and the tyrant's rage—
The glorious father of the glorious age.

Unclouded rapture smiles on every face,
As joyful thousands by their guardian pass:
O'er all the scene his eye with pleasure roves.
And drops the tear while the procession moves.

Round the wide world his mighty name shall grow,
As far as oceans roll, or winds can blow,
And to remotest future time be known,
His virtues—God like deeds—and high renown.

—*Boston Gazette*, 30 November 1789.

# "He Comes, He Comes to Boston"

## ODE
### Upon the Arrival of THE PRESIDENT OF THE UNITED STATES.

*Ut* mater juvenem, *quem Notus invido*
*Flatu Carpathu trans maris æquora*
*Cunctantium spatio longius annuo*
  *Dulci distinct a domo,*
Votis, ominibusque, et precibus vocat;
*Curvo nec faciem littore demovet;*
Sic desideriis icta fidelibus
  Quærit patria *WASHINGTON.*
                              HORACE.

### *RECITATIVE.*
He comes! the Hero comes! tis He!
Who gave to *Howe* this high decree,
"Avaunt—Begone."—He bow'd—He fled;
And hallow'd Freedom rais'd her head,
Where *Clinton* shook th' avenging rod,
And round thy courts, Almighty God!
*Burgoyne*, by impious phrenzy driven,
Taught the war steed to mock at Heaven.

### *AIR.*
Massachusetts Arise!
Seize the Trumpet of Fame,
Tone it loud—and proclaim,
Glorious WASHINGTON's name,
  The first born of the skies!

### *RECITATIVE.*
He comes! the Chieftain comes! All hail!

'Twas his on *Trenton's* crimson'd vale—
And *Princeton's* lawn—and *Brandywine*,
To whelm in dust *Britannia's* line;
'Twas his, to lead *Columbia's* train
To deathless deeds, on *Monmouth's* plain;
Or bid the storm of battle cease,
When proud *Cornwallis* su'd for peace.

### AIR.

Swell the pæan divine;
Earth repeat it again!
Ocean echo the strain!
Heaven thunder amen!
Columbia! GEORGE WASHINGTON's thine!

### RECITATIVE.

He comes! the Patriot comes! 'tis he!
Who fought to make his country free;
Whom no ambition fir'd to arms;
And when the clarion's shrill alarms,
Rous'd not in wrath an angry world,
Laid by those bolts which virtue hurl'd,
And bade unconquer'd legions turn,
From war's rude mound—to concord's bourne.

### AIR.

Heroes! mark his retreat!
Fair abode! beauteous clime!
Second Eden of time!
Is great WASHINGTON's seat!

### RECITATIVE.

He comes! He comes! He comes! 'Tis He!
Kings! Princes! Nations! bow the knee!
Ye worlds! pronounce, "Thy will be done:"
The patriot Hero WASHINGTON!
Above a Crown—a Scepter—Throne,
Rules in the heart supreme—alone,

And millions leagu'd in love's strong chain,
United shout—God *bless his reign.*

### GRAND CHORUS.

Glorious WASHINGTON sway!
    All the realms of the west,
    And in blessing, he blest,
    Till th' *Eternal's* behest
Shall summon thy subjects away;
    Then call'd to the sky,
    Sacred virtue's abode!
    Reign forever with GOD!
    In the mansions on high!
*Boston, October,* 1789.          G.R.

—*Massachusetts Magazine,* October 1789. Reprinted in the
*Gazette of the United States,* 18 November, and the Lan-
singburgh, New York, *Federal Herald,* 30 November.
Throughout the poem references are made to battles in
the Revolution and to British generals William Howe,
Henry Clinton, John Burgoyne, and Charles Cornwallis.

# "The Godlike Washington"

(*The following* ODE *was composed to be sung on
the arrival of* THE PRESIDENT.)

### O D E.

See the man! *Columbia's* son!
See the godlike WASHINGTON!
Let the grateful, cheerful lay,
Hail this bright, auspicious day.

CHORUS.—*See the man!* Columbia's *son!*
*See the godlike* WASHINGTON!

When *Bellona* urg'd her car,
Then he rose, the strength of war;
Now, when *Peace* adorns our plains,
Still his mighty hand sustains.
CHORUS.—*See the man! &c.*

Valour here, and Wisdom meet,
The plan of Empire to complete;
Now the glorious task is done,
Hail the Victor, WASHINGTON.
CHORUS.—*See the man! &c.*

—*Massachusetts Centinel*, 7 November 1789.

# ODE TO THE PRESIDENT OF THE UNITED STATES.

### BY A LADY.

### The MUSICK set by Mr. HANS GRAM.

Allegro moderato.

The season sheds its mildest ray, O'er the blue waves the sunbeams play, The bending harvest gilds the plain, The tow'ring vessels press the main, The ruddy ploughman quits his toil, The pallid miser leaves his spoil, And grateful pæans hail the smiling year, Which bids Columbia's Guardian God appear.

### Chorus.

And grateful pæans hail the smiling year, Which bids Columbia's Guardian God appear.

[*The four bars in the last line belong to the four parts of the Chorus; one bar to each part; the first bar to the Treble; second to the Counter; third to the Tenor; and the last to the Bass.*]

From the *Massachusetts Magazine*, October 1789, pp. 660-61.

# "Matchless Deeds"

## ⚔ ⚔

### *O D E* to THE PRESIDENT—
BY A LADY.

#### I.

The season sheds its mildest ray,
O'er the blue waves the sun-beams play;
The bending harvest gilds the plain,
The towering vessels press the main;
The ruddy ploughman quits his toil.
The pallid miser leaves his spoil;
And grateful Pæans hail the smiling year,
Which bids *Columbia's* guardian Chief appear.

#### II.

Hence! disappointment's anxious eye,
And pale affliction's lingering sigh!
Let beaming Hope the brow adorn,
And every heart forget to mourn;
Let smiles of Peace their charms display,
To grace this joy-devoted day:
And where *that* arm preserv'd the peopled plain,
Shall mild Contentment hold her placid reign.

#### III.

Let "*white-rob'd choirs,*" in beauty gay,
With lucid flowers strew the way;
Let roses deck the scented lawn,
And Lilach lift their purple form;
Let Domes in circling honours spread,
And wreaths adorn that glorious head;
To thee, GREAT WASHINGTON, each lyre be
    strung!
Thy matchless deeds by every Bard be sung!

163

## IV.

When *Freedom* rais'd her drooping head,
Thy arm her willing heroes led;
And when *her* hopes, to thee resign'd,
Were resting on thy God-like mind,
How did *that* breast, to fear unknown,
And feeling for *her* fate alone,
O'er Danger's threat'ning form the Faulchion wield,
And tread with dauntless step the crimson'd field.

## V.

Not DECIUS[1]—for his country slain,
Nor CINCINNATUS—deathless name!
CAMILLUS[2]—who could wrongs despise,
And, scorning wealth, to glory rise,
Could such exalted worth display,
Or shine with such *unclouded* ray:
Of *age* the *hope*, of *youth* the *leading star*,
THE SOUL OF PEACE, THE CONQUERING ARM OF WAR.

—*Massachusetts Centinel*, 31 October 1789. Reprinted in
the *Providence Gazette*, 7 November; the *Gazette of the
United States*, 11 November; *New Hampshire Gazette*, 11
November; Philadelphia *Federal Gazette*, 14 November;
*Pennsylvania Gazette*, 18 November; and the November
issue of the Philadelphia *American Museum*. The music
was printed in the October 1789 issue of the *Massachusetts
Magazine*.

[1]Publius Decius Mus, the name of three generations of Roman
consuls who sacrificed themselves to assure victory in the Samnite
War (340 B.C.–279 B.C.).
[2]Marcus Furius Camillus (d. 365 B.C.) defeated the city of Veii
after a ten-year war and saved Rome from complete destruction by
Gallic invasion.

# A "Gratulary Song"

An ODE *performed at the* ORATORIO *in the* STONE-CHAPEL, *on Tuesday last* [27 October].[1]

RECITATIVE.

Behold the man! whom virtues raise,
   The highest of the patriot throng!
To him the muse her homage pays,
   And tunes the gratulary song.


AIR.

Illustrious Visitant! design'd
   By Heaven's invincible decree,
T' enoble and exalt the mind,
   And teach a nation to be free.


Welcome, thrice welcome to the spot,
   Where once thy conq'ring banners wav'd,
O never be thy praise forgot,
   By those thy matchless valour sav'd.


Thy glory beams to *Eastern* skies,
   See! Europe shares the sacred flame—
And hosts of patriot heroes rise,
   To emulate thy glorious name.

[1]On 27 October Washington attended the Stone-Chapel to hear a concert of sacred music which was to be preceded by the foregoing ode to him. The full oratorio was not performed on 27 October because "several Singers" were ill with influenza. "Several pieces were however given, which merited and received applause." On 25 November the *Massachusetts Centinel* announced that a full performance would be held on 1 December, "if the weather permits, otherwise on the next day." Tickets were available at two shillings each.

Labor awhile suspends his toil,
　His debt of gratitude to pay;
And friendship wears a brighter smile;
　And Musick breathes a sweeter lay.

May health and joy a wreath entwine,
　And guard thee thro' this scene of strife;
'Till seraphs shall to thee assign,
　A wreath of everlasting life.

—*Massachusetts Centinel*, 31 October 1789. Reprinted in
the *Gazette of the United States*, 4 November; *New York
Packet*, 7 November; Philadelphia *Federal Gazette*, 7 November; *Newport Herald*, 12 November; Baltimore *Maryland Gazette*, 13 November; Lansingburgh, New York,
*Federal Herald*, 16 November; Charleston, S.C., *City Gazette*, 5 December. It was also printed as a broadside.

# An Old Soldier Recollected

A number of singular incidents occurred during the
late tour of the President, which give him much satisfaction—Among others, was the following. On his
arrival at Newbury-Port, a poor old soldier, by the
name of *Cotton*, commonly called *Colonel*, who was in
the memorable battle, when BRADOCK was defeated on
the banks of the Ohio,[1] and served under the President,
who was then a Major, requested, and was admitted
into the room where the President was—On the soldier's bowing, and asking *"how Major Washington did,"*

[1]General Edward Braddock's forces were defeated by the
French and Indians in 1755 near Fort Duquesne. Braddock, who was
mortally wounded, lost over half of his force.

the President immediately recollecting his person, and rising from his chair, took him by the hand and tenderly inquired into the scenes of his life, and present circumstances—"I thank God," answered the soldier "that I have an opportunity of seeing my old Commander once more. I have seen him in adversity, and now seeing him in glory, I can go home and die contented." The next morning he came again, to take his leave of the President, who gave him a guinea, which he accepted, he said, "merely as a token in remembrance of his Commander," and which he now wears pendant on his bosom, declaring that nothing earthly shall separate it from him.

—*Massachusetts Centinel*, 25 November 1789.

# *No Need For Titles*

娶 娶

The PRESIDENT of United America will arrive in town this day.
IMPROMPTO *on the Approach of the* PRESIDENT *of the* UNITED STATES.
—Fame stretch'd her wings, and with her trumpet blew,
Great WASHINGTON, is near:—What praise *his* due!
What Titles shall HE have? She paus'd and said,
Not one; HIS NAME alone strikes every Title dead.

—*New Hampshire Spy*, 31 October 1789. Reprinted in the Hartford *American Mercury*, 9 November; *New York Journal*, 19 November; and in the November issue of the Philadelphia *American Museum*.

# Welcome to Newburyport

Friday last [30 October] the beloved President of the United States made his entry into this town and never did a person appear here, who more largely shared the affection and esteem of its citizens. He was escorted here by two companies of cavalry from Ipswich and Andover. On his drawing near he was saluted with 13 discharges from the artillery; after which a number of young gentlemen placed themselves before him and sung as follows:—

He comes! He comes! the HERO comes!
Sound, sound your trumpets, beat, beat your drums;
From port, to port, let cannon roar
He's welcome to New-England's shore!
    Welcome, welcome, welcome, welcome,
    Welcome to New-England's shore!

Prepare! prepare! your songs prepare,
Loud, loudly rend the echoing air;
From pole to pole, his praise resound,
For virtue is with glory crown'd!
    Virtue, virtue, virtue, virtue,
    Virtue is with glory crown'd!

The lines in the first verse which call for the beating of drums and roaring of cannon, were instantly obeyed after the pronunciation of each word; and to the vocal was joined all the instrumental music in both choruses, which were repeated.—Then the President preceded by the several companies of militia and artillery of this town, the select men, High Sherif, and Marshal Jackson passed the ministers, physicians, lawyers, magistrates, town officers, marine society, cap-

tains of vessels, sailors, schoolmasters with their scholars, &c. who had paraded and opened to the right and
left, for that purpose, each of whom as the President
passed, closed and joined in the procession, which was
terminated by about 420 scholars, all with their quills
in their hands, headed by their preceptors.—Their motto,
"*WE are the Free-born subjects of the United States.*"

—Newburyport, Mass., *Essex Journal*, 4 November 1789.
Reprinted in the *New York Weekly Museum*, 14 November
1789; the *Gazette of the United States*, 14 November; *New
York Journal*, 19 November; and the *Pennsylvania Packet*,
19 November. The poem was modified and used in the
Charleston, S.C., ceremonies on 2 May 1791. See "General
Eclat and Splendor in Charleston," below.

# *Hantonia*[1] *Hosts the President*

豕 豕

## ARRIVAL of his Excellency the PRESIDENT
## of the UNITED STATES.

On Saturday last [31 October], arrived in this Metropolis [Portsmouth], his Excellency GEORGE WASHING-
TON, Esq. President of the United States of America.

His Excellency was met at the line by the President
[John Sullivan] and Council of this State—several members of the Hon. House of Representatives—the Honorable Messieurs Langdon and Wingate, Senators for
this State—the Hon. Nicholas Gilman, Esq. the Treasurer of this State—the Loan Officer—the Marshal and
Attorney of this District, the Hon. Consul of France,

[1]New Hampshire.

169

the Secretary of this State, several General Officers, attended by Col. Cogswell, with his regiment of Light-Horse, in complete uniform—a respectable number of officers in the Civil Department, and private gentlemen.

The President was escorted to the line by a party of horse from our sister state, and was there introduced, in form, to the several gentlemen of distinction who were waiting his arrival. He then passed the troops drawn up to receive him; who severally vied with each other, who could pay the most respect to the man whom heaven approves, and Americans delight to honour. The President then dismounted from his horse, took his carriage and was escorted to Greenland. The way, for the most part, being lined with spectators of all ranks. At Greenland he was met by Colonel Wentworth's corps of Independent Horse (in complete uniform, having their standard displayed, as were the standards of the several corps) many more officers of the militia, and several gentlemen from this and the neighbouring towns. The President after a short tarry at Greenland, re-mounted his horse, and passed the officers who were drawn up near the Globe Tavern, under the command of the Hon. Major-General Cilley, to salute him as he passed.

At his entrance into this town he was saluted by thirteen cannon from three companies of Artillery, in complete uniform, under the command of Col. Hacket. The street through which he passed (Congress Street) was lined by the citizens of the town, all the crafts being ranged alphabetically; the Bells rang a joyful peal, and repeated shouts from grateful thousands, hail'd their Deliverer welcome to the Metropolis of New-Hampshire.

*Then did the people's just applauses rise,*
*And the loud shout ran echoing thro' the states.*

A federal Salute was fired from the Castle, the ships in the harbour were dressed, and the windows and doors of every house were crowded with ladies, anxious to see and bless the man to whom America stands so much indebted.

On his arrival at the State-House, he was conducted to the Senate Chamber, by the President and Council of this State, and took his station in the balcony, when in a stage erected for the purpose, the following Odes, composed by a gentleman in this town, were sung by a number of gentlemen, accompanied by the band:

## ODE FIRST.

### FULL CHORUS.
Behold he comes! Columbia's pride,
And Nature's boast—her fav'rite Son,
Of valour—wisdom—truth—well try'd—
Hail, Matchless WASHINGTON.

### RECITATIVE.
*'Tis gratitude that prompts the humble lay,*
*Accept great Chief what Gratitude can pay.*

### AIR.
Let old and young—let rich and poor,
Their voices raise,
To sing his praise,
And bid him welcome o'er and o'er.

### CHORUS.
*Welcome matchless WASHINGTON!*
*Matchless as the deeds you've done.*

### RECITATIVE.
*From North to South, from East to West*
*His Fame unrival'd stands confest.*

### AIR.
This, this is he—by Heaven design'd,
The pride and wonder of mankind.

United then your voices raise,
And all united sing his praise.

## CHORUS.
*Welcome matchless WASHINGTON!*
*Matchless as the deeds you've done.*

## ODE SECOND.
*Tune——"He comes"*

He comes! he comes! your songs prepare,
The matchless Chief approaches near,
Each heart exults! each tongue proclaims,
He's welcome to *Hantonia's* plains.

## CHORUS.
*Welcome! welcome! welcome! welcome!*
*Welcome to Hantonia's plains.*
Those shouts ascending to the sky,
Proclaim great WASHINGTON is nigh!
Hail nature's boast—Columbia's Son,
Welcome! welcome WASHINGTON.
*Welcome! &c.*
Let strains harmonious rend the air.
For see the Godlike hero's here!
Thrice hail—Columbia's fav'rite Son.
Thrice welcome matchless WASHINGTON.
*Welcome, &c.*

## ODE THIRD.
*Tune——"God save the King."*

Long may thy Trumpet, Fame,
Let echo waft the Name,
Of WASHINGTON:
O'er all the world around,
Far as earth's utmost bound,
Thy equal is not found,
Columbia's Son.

## II.

Ye blest of Human kind.
Columbians, call to mind,
    Th' deeds he's done:
Hark! hark! those shouts declare,
That "Heaven's peculiar care,"
The matchless Hero's here,
    Great WASHINGTON.

## III.

*Hantonia's* sons rejoice,
Welcome with heart and voice,
    Your country's pride:
On this auspicious day,
Drive sorrow far away,
And sing in rapt'rous lay,
    "Let joy preside."

## IV.

Rejoice—let all rejoice,
And with united voice,
    The HERO hail;
He stem'd oppression's tide,
And humbled Britain's pride,
Is still your matchless guide
    That will not fail.

Then the whole of the troops, under the command of Major-General Cilley, passed him in the review, Horse, Foot and Artillery, and the line of Officers, every Officer saluting as he passed. The Troops then retired, and the President was conducted to his lodgings, at Col. Brewster's, by the President and Council of this State, the Hon. Mr. Langdon and the Marshall of this district, escorted by a company under arms, and in complete uniform.

Every thing was conducted with the greatest possible order and regularity, each countenance beamed with lively joy—sorrow was banished far away, and each heart beat grateful to the name of WASHINGTON.

In the evening, the State-House was beautifully illuminated—thirteen rockets were let off the balcony—mutual gratulations took place, and the day concluded without any unlucky occurrence to mar the pleasure excited by so auspicious an event. Thus far for the day—we flatter ourselves it will be remembered so long as patriotism continues to be a virtue, and the name of WASHINGTON to sound grateful to American ears.

—*New Hampshire Gazette*, 5 November 1789. Reprinted in the Boston *Independent Chronicle*, 12 November; the *Gazette of the United States*, 14 November; and the Lansingburgh, New York, *Federal Herald*, 23 November.

# "The Chieftain Comes"

There could not have been an observation made with more truth, than that our beloved PRESIDENT "unites all hearts and all voices in his favour;" and his late visit into the Eastern States has fully demonstrated it. At his approach, party disappears; and every one runs a race in endeavouring who shall be foremost in paying him the tribute of grateful respect. Old and young—men and women—all, all are alike affected—and all alike endeavour to express their feelings by the most lively testimonials—language has been found inadequate to express the joy of our citizens, the delineation of which has been *attempted* in their addresses: And although the subject has added inspiration to the votaries of the Muses, yet they have been necessitated to own, that *"expressive silence"* alone can sing his worth.

Although the season has been inauspicious—yet that

has been no obstruction to thousands from thronging the streets—climbing

> *"On walls and towers—yea to chimney tops,*
> *Their infants in their arms—and there have sat*
> *The live-long day, in patient expectation*
> *To see their* Guardian *as he pass'd along."*

And even now all ranks appear constrained to own, that they have not paid their debt of gratitude.

ILLUSTRIOUS PATRIOT—our obligations to thee are infinite—but you have a recompense in the reflection that your country has approved your conduct, and that you reign in the hearts of every individual of your fellow citizens—who are as proud to own their obligations, as it is impossible to forget the services which demand them. In peace and war your abilities have been found adequate to every exigency—and on your approach, your fellow-citizens recognizing them, with united voices, proclaim,

> *"He comes! the Chieftain comes! all hail,*
> *'Twas yours on* Trenton's *crimson'd vale—*
> *And* Princeton's *lawn—and* Brandywine
> *To whelm in dust* Brittania's *line.*
> *'Twas yours to lead Columbia's train*
> *To deathless deeds, on* Monmouth's *plain,*
> *Or bid the storm of battle cease,*
> *When proud* CORNWALLIS *su'd for peace."*
> *"Above a Crown—a Sceptre—Throne*
> *Rule in our hearts—supreme—alone.*
> *For millions leagu'd in love's strong chain,*
> *United shout—*GOD *bless your reign."*[1]

AN AMERICAN.

—*Massachusetts Centinel*, 7 November 1789.

[1]These lines were quoted and paraphrased from the *Massachusetts Magazine*, October 1789. See "He Comes, He Comes To Boston," above.

# Spontaneous Joy

… Yesterday [13 November] the illustrious PRES-
IDENT of the United States, arrived in town [New
York], from his tour through the Eastern States. His
arrival was immediately announced by a discharge of
cannon from the fort.

The attention and respect shewn to our beloved
President by the Magistrates of the several States
through which he has passed, while they were tributes
justly due to the Chief Magistrate of the Union, demonstrate that there exists a perfect cordiality between
the Federal and State Officers,—a circumstance which
must give infinite pleasure to every friend to his country, and added to the universal attachment of the people,
is evincive of their esteem for the federal government—
as they all emphatically say,

> Long rest the sceptre in his *equal* hand.
> And to his trust may Heaven propitious be,
> Long may he rule a willing land:
> And oh! FOREVER MAY THAT LAND BE FREE.

It is related of Mahomet, in the legends of his religion, that wherever he trod, flowers spontaneously
arose. This *dream* of oriental flattery, appears to be
more than realized in the progress of our beloved President—for wherever he proceeded, joy, gratitude, affection, veneration and love, sprang spontaneously in
the hearts of all ages, and of all conditions of his fellow-
citizens.

—*Massachusetts Centinel*, 21 November 1789. Reprinted
from a New York newspaper of 14 November (not found).

# A United People

Yesterday [13 November], at one o'clock, THE PRESIDENT of the United States returned to this city [New York] in perfect health, from his tour thro the Eastern States.

This event was announced by a federal salute from the Battery.

THE PRESIDENT left Portsmouth last week on Wednesday—his route was thro *Exeter, Haverhill, Lexington, Watertown, etc.* to *Hartford.*

There is a variety of incidents that attend the tour of the President, which must fill every patriotic mind with peculiar pleasure: Independent of that personal respect which is paid to him as a Man, there is an invariable reference in all the addresses, to his political situation, and that Constitution over whose administration he presides. These national sentiments are universally reiterated—and plainly prove that the people are united in their hopes and expectations of public freedom, peace and happiness from the general government.

The time to pull down, and destroy, is now past— As it was ONCE designative of the highest patriotism to overturn those systems which were found incompatible with that Independence which the United States had assumed—so NOW it is equally their duty to build up, strengthen and support a Constitution, with which is inseparably connected all that is dear and valuable to us as citizens and freemen. This sentiment appears to pervade the minds of the people, and must strengthen the hands, and encourage the hearts of our civil rulers, while it inspires with pleasure the hearts of every real friend to the United States.

—*Gazette of the United States*, 14 November 1789.

# "Demonstrative Evidence of What the People Feel"

茇 茇

*Extract of a letter from Boston, to the Editor hereof,*
*dated November 3.*

The President hath visited us—"All his steps were dignity and love"—It was glorious at once to embrace our Friend and Brother—Fellow Citizen—General—Supreme Magistrate—Political Father—Head of our Nation—and Representative of the Majesty of the United States—whose virtues are a blessing to the world.—Every pulse seemed to beat ardor for his welfare—every heart was animated—and most sincere were our efforts to pay him respect—and make him happy.—My confinement by severe indisposition, the day after his arrival, and during his residence here, deprived me of the pleasure of paying my personal respects to him—This was a great *draw back* upon my happiness on the glorious occasion.

The tour of THE PRESIDENT thro the Eastern States is an event, which has served to call forth the latent principles of virtue, gratitude, and patriotism, in an eminent degree:—The real friends to the revolution—the advocates for government, peace, and freedom, were fully convinced that the attachment of the people to the Constitution was solid and permanent—that their love and veneration for the President could receive no addition—Still the pen of slander has not been idle—and the tongue of calumny has not been silent—while jealousies and apprehensions have been excited respecting imaginary evils—It therefore seemed necessary that some great occasion should offer, to call forth the real sentiments of the Union, and afford that demonstrative evidence of what the people *feel*, which all the adversaries of our national honor "should not be able to gainsay or resist."

—*Gazette of the United States*, 18 November 1789.

# "To Bigotry No Sanction— To Persecution No Assistance"

🗡 🗡

AN ADDRESS.
*To the* PRESIDENT *of the* UNITED STATES *of* AMERICA.

Sir, Permit the Children of the Stock of Abraham to approach you with the most cordial affection and esteem for your person and merits—and to join with our fellow-citizens in welcoming you to Newport.

With pleasure we reflect on those days—those days of difficulty and danger, when the GOD of Israel, who delivered David from the peril of the sword—shielded your head in the day of battle:—And we rejoice to think, that the same spirit, who rested in the bosom of the greatly beloved Daniel, enabling him to preside over the provinces of the Babylonish Empire, rests, and ever will rest, upon you, enabling you to discharge the arduous duties of CHIEF MAGISTRATE in these States.

Deprived as we heretofore have been of the invaluable rights of free citizens, we now (with a deep sense of gratitude to the Almighty Disposer of all events) behold a Government erected by the MAJESTY OF THE PEOPLE—a Government which to bigotry gives no sanction—to persecution no assistance; but generously affording to ALL liberty of conscience, and immunities of citizenship—deeming every one, of whatever nation, tongue, or language, equal parts of the great governmental machine. This so ample and extensive Federal Union, whose basis is philanthropy, mutual confidence, and public virtue, we cannot but acknowledge to be the work of the Great GOD, who ruleth in the armies of heaven and among the inhabitants of the earth, doing whatsoever seemeth him good.

For all the blessings of civil and religious liberty which we enjoy under an equal and benign administration, we desire to send up our thanks to the Ancient of Days, the great Preserver of men—beseeching him, that the Angel who conducted our forefathers through the wilderness into the promised land, may graciously conduct you through all the difficulties and dangers of this mortal life; and when, like Joshua, full of days and full of honor, you are gathered to your Fathers, may you be admitted into the Heavenly Paradise to partake of the water of life, and the tree of immortality.

*Done and signed by order of the* Hebrew Congregation, *in* Newport, *Rhode-island, August* 17, 1790.

MOSES SEIXAS, Warden.


THE PRESIDENT's ANSWER.
*To the* HEBREW CONGREGATION *in* Newport, RHODE-ISLAND.

Gentlemen, While I receive with much satisfaction, your Address replete with expressions of affection and esteem, I rejoice in the opportunity of assuring you, that I shall always retain a grateful remembrance of the cordial welcome I experienced in my visit to Newport, from all classes of citizens.

The reflection on the days of difficulty and danger which are past, is rendered the more sweet, from a consciousness that they are succeeded by days of uncommon prosperity and security. If we have wisdom to make the best use of the advantages with which we are now favored, we cannot fail, under the just administration of a good government, to become a great and a happy people.

The citizens of the United States of America, have a right to applaud themselves for having given to mankind examples of an enlarged and liberal policy—a policy worthy of imitation. ALL possess alike liberty of conscience, and immunities of citizenship. It is now no more that toleration is spoken of, as if it was by the indulgence of one class of people, that another enjoyed the exercise of their inherent natural rights. For happily the government of the United States, which gives to bigotry no sanction—to persecution no assistance, requires only that they who live under its protection should demean themselves as good citizens, in giving it on all occasions their effectual support.

It would be inconsistent with the frankness of my character not to avow, that I am pleased with your favorable opinion of my administration, and fervent wishes for my felicity. May the Children of the Stock of Abraham, who dwell in this land, continue to merit and enjoy the good-will of the other inhabitants; while every one shall sit in safety under his own vine and fig-tree, and there shall be none to make him afraid. May the Father of all mercies scatter light and not darkness in our paths, and make us all in our several vocations useful here, and in his own due time and way everlastingly happy.

Geo. Washington.

—*Newport Herald*, 9 September 1790. Reprinted in newspapers throughout the country.

# Saved Again

🦅 🦅

Early on Friday morning last [25 March 1791], this city [Annapolis] was honoured by the arrival of The PRESIDENT, attended by only his private secretary, Major Jackson. Intelligence having been received of his intended embarkation at Rock Hall, he had been anxiously expected on Thursday evening—but the governor [John Eager Howard], and several other gentlemen, who had sailed to meet him, were compelled to return without tidings. The vessel, which contained the chief treasure of America, did not enter the river Severn until ten o'clock, in a dark, tempestuous night. She struck on a bar, or point, within about a mile of this city; and although she made a signal of distress, it was impossible, before day-light, to go to her relief.[1] The guardian angel of America was still watchful; and we are happy in assuring our countrymen that the health of their dearest friend has not been at all affected by an accident far

[1]Washington described his journey to Annapolis in his diary: "Unluckily, embarking on board of a borrowed Boat because She was the largest, I was in imminent danger, from the unskilfulness of the hands, and the dulness of her sailing, added to the darkness and storminess of the night. For two hours after we hoisted Sail the Wind was light and a head. The next hour was a stark calm after which the wind sprung up at So. Et. and encreased until it blew a gale—about which time, and after 8 Oclock P.M. we made the mouth of Severn River (leading up to Annapolis) but the ignorance of the People on board, with respect to the navigation of it run us aground first on Greenbury point from whence with much exertion and difficulty we got off; & then, having no knowledge of the Channel and the night being immensely dark with heavy and variable squals of wind—constant lightning & tremendous thunder—we soon grounded again on what is called Hornes point where, finding all efforts in vain, &, not knowing where we were we remained, not knowing what might happen, 'till morning."

more distressing to those who were apprised, or rather apprehensive, of his situation, than to himself.

At 10 o'clock on the same day, attended by the governor, and a number of respectable citizens, he visited the college [St. Johns], and expressed much satisfaction at the appearance of this rising seminary—He then pursued his walk to the government house. At three o'clock he sat down to a public dinner at Mr. Mann's[2] with a numerous company of the inhabitants, and continued at table until there had been circulated the following toasts, each of which was announced by the discharge of cannon—

1. The People of the United States of America.
2. The Congress.
3. The dearest Friend of his Country.
4. The State of Maryland.
5. Wisdom, Justice and Harmony, in all our Public Councils.
6. Agriculture, Manufactures, Commerce and Learning; may they flourish with Virtue and true Religion.
7. The King of the French.
8. The National Assembly of France.
9. The Sieur la Fayette, and the other generous Friends to America in the day of her Distress.
10. The Memory of all those who have fallen in the Cause of America.
11. The Patriots of all Nations and Ages.
12. The Powers of Europe friendly to America.
13. May all the Inhabitants of the Earth be taught to consider each other as Fellow-Citizens.
14. The Virtuous Daughters of America.
15. The perpetual Union of distinct Sovereign States under an efficient Federal Head.

On Saturday the President again dined with a large company at the government house; and in the evening

---

[2]Mann's Tavern, site of the Annapolis Convention.

183

his presence enlivened a ball, at which was exhibited every thing which this little city contains of beauty and elegance.

It is no exaggeration to declare, that, during two days, all care seemed suspended; and the inhabitants of a whole town were made happy in contemplating him whom they consider as their safest friend, as well as the most exalted of their fellow-citizens, and the first of men.

On Sunday, at eight o'clock, he rode out of town, attended by a company of gentlemen, of whom he took leave at South river. The governor waits on him to George-Town, where he purposes to remain some days before he pursues his arduous patriotic journey to the southward.

—Annapolis *Maryland Gazette*, 31 March 1791. The first paragraph was reprinted in the Edenton *State Gazette of North Carolina*, 22 April.

# "A Hero Great and Good"

When the president of the united states of America honored, with his presence, the examination of the students of the Richmond Academy, the following address was delivered by master Edmund Bacon, with such distinctness of articulation; such propriety of pauses and emphasies; and in a manner so truly pathetic, as to keep that illustrious hero and a numerous collection of gentlemen in tears almost the whole time the little orator was speaking.

In ages past, we see a splendid train
Of heroes shine, in panegyric's strain.
Historic pens have varnish'd o'er their crimes,
And prais'd, in them, the vices of the times:
To conquer nations; millions to devour;
To reign in all the wantonness of power;
To follow glory; to acquire a name;
Their cause ambition, and their object fame.
'Tis ours to boast a hero great and good;
With courage and *benevolence* endued.

Superior genious! you, whose breast can feel
No other motive but your country's weal.
Superior firmness! with such virtues arm'd;
By power, untainted,—by no flattery charm'd.
Superior chief! by selfish views unmov'd;
Your people loving, by your people lov'd.
Let not th' expressions of our love offend
Our saviour, father, citizen and friend.
Deny us not the pleasure thus t' impart,
Without disguise, the feelings of the heart.

Thou friend of science, liberty, and laws,
Forever active in thy country's cause;
We are thy children—let thy fancy trace,
In us, the congregated, rising race—
Adopted, ere we drew the vital air,
And snatch'd from slavery by thy watchful care.
Heirs of that freedom, by that valor won;
May we ne'er mar the work by thee begun!
As we've been taught to glow at thy renown,
So we'd transmit by bright example down.
Each future babe shall learn to lisp thy name;[1]
To love thy worth and emulate thy fame.
When'er the powers of infant reason dawn,
Full in his view thy portrait shall be drawn.
Hence on his mind these truths will be impress'd;
That virtue only can be truly blest.

[1]See Chapter III, "Beyond Raphael's Description," note i.

Though power may glare in all the pomp of state;
That virtue only can be truly great,
Though vanity may bask in flattery's rays;
That virtue only meets with honest praise:
That virtue only claims our whole esteem;
That virtue only reigns with power supreme.

In our full hearts, what grateful rise!
When, o'er past scenes, our active fancy flies:
We hail the day, you took the glorious field,
And made the haughty British Lion yield!
Then, though a scepter waited on your word,
For calm retirement, you resign'd the sword,
You scorn'd the glory power usurp'd imparts;
You scorn'd to reign but in a people's heart.
Again we see you bless Potomack's shore,
Resolv'd to leave sweet Vernon's shades no more.
Delightful seat! by your fond choice design'd,
T'enjoy, in peace, your self approving mind.
Again your country call'd you to her aid;
And you again your country's call obey'd.
With fond regret, you left your fav'rite shore,
To feel the weight of public cares once more.

Hail joyous day! what acclamations rung!
Joy fill'd each eye, and rapture mov'd each tongue,
At your instalment!—never monarch wore
So bright, so rich a diadem before.
No more let sparkling dross ambition move;
Your diadem, is—*universal love*.

But hold—this theme is painfull to your ear:
Though lightly touch'd, by gratitude sincere—
Indulge our joys, forgive our forward zeal;
Let your own heart imagine what we feel!
What various transports in our bosoms glow,
Swell the full heart, and at the eyes o'erflow!!—

Almighty God! Since virtue is thy care;—
O hear a nation's universal prayer!
May all the joys, this transient scene can know,
Full on his heart, in gentle currents, flow!—

May all the joys, benevolence inspires,
Pursue him still when he from time retires!—
May this one joy, forever crown the whole;
And with immortal rapture fill his soul!
May he, from heaven's sublime, eternal scenes,
See future millions happy through his means!!!—
    And let mankind this serious truth confess;
None e'er was prais'd so much,—none ever flatter'd
    less.

—*South-Carolina Independent Gazette*, 25 June 1791. Reprinted in the *Augusta Chronicle*, 4 June 1791 (supplement). Washington arrived in Richmond on 11 April and left on the 14th.

# *Praised in Petersburg*

On Thursday last [14 April 1791] arrived in this town, the President of the United States, accompanied by his private secretary, Major Jackson. The President was escorted into town by the cavalry of Chesterfield, Prince-George, and Dinwiddie, and a considerable number of citizens, and conducted to the house of Robert Armistead, where an elegant entertainment was provided, at which the President was pleased to favor the citizens with his presence. After dinner a number of patriotic toasts were drank attended by a discharge of cannon; next in the evening the President was pleased to accept an invitation to a ball at the Masons Hall. A committee from the Commons Hall waited on the President with the following address. The next morning, at 5 o'clock, the President proceeded on his tour to the southward, by way of Halifax, N. Carolina.

The ADDRESS of the Mayor, Recorder, Aldermen, and Common Council, of the town of PETERSBURG. To the President of the United States.

Sir, We avail ourselves of the earliest opportunity that your presence has afforded us, to offer you our sincere and affectionate respects; to welcome you, most cordially, to this place, and to assure you, which we do with confidence, of the high regard and great affection the inhabitants of this town entertain for your person, and your many virtues. We look upon you, Sir, as the father of your country, and the friend of mankind, and when we contemplate your character in that light, we feel ourselves impressed with the purest sentiments of gratitude, respect and veneration. May you long continue at the head of our government, honoured, respected and beloved, as you are at present; and we pray, most ardently, that the all-wise Director of human events, may prolong your life to a far distant period of time, and may bless you to your latest breath, with health uninterrupted, and with that happy tranquility of mind which ever flows from a conscious rectitude, and from a heart always anxious to promote the happiness of the human race.

We sincerely wish that the tour which you are about to make, may be an agreeable one, and that it may afford you every imaginable satisfaction.

Joseph Westmore, Mayor.

—Fredericksburg *Virginia Herald*, 28 April 1791.

# "A Sincere Love of Liberty" Elevates a Nation

🐉 🐉

To the President of the United States
From the Inhabitants of Newbern—

Sir, With hearts impressed with the most lively emotions of Love, Esteem and Veneration, We meet you at this time to express the joy We feel in your visit to the State of North Carolina.

We Sympathize with You in those delightful sensations, which you now so fully experience when We reflect with you on our past difficulties and dangers during a long and arduous War, and contrast these with the bright, the glorious prospects which present themselves of our beloved Country's enjoying in perfect peace, the inestimable blessings of Civil and Religious Liberty.

Our Souls overflow with gratitude to the bountiful Dispenser of all good Gifts, that He has committed to your hands the reins of Government in that Country during peace, of which you have been so lately the defence against the Arm of Despotism and Arbitrary Sway.—

May Almighty God prolong that Life, which has been so eminently useful to the Human Race, for it is not America Alone—but the World shall learn from your example to what a stupendous height of Glory, a Nation may be elevated—whose freeborn souls are fired with a sincere love of LIBERTY.—

It is our most earnest Prayer to the throne of Heavenly Grace that the divine Benediction may accompany you here and hereafter.

> —Washington Papers, Library of Congress. The address, presented to Washington on 22 April 1791, was signed by Joseph Leech, James Coor, John Sitgreaves, Ben Williams, Dan Carthy, William McClure, Saml. Chapman, and Isaac Guion.

# General Eclat and Splendor in Charleston

☙ ☙

## THE PRESIDENT's ARRIVAL

On Monday the 2d inst. [2 May 1791] at 2 o'clock,
P.M. the beloved and excellent GEORGE WASHING-
TON, Esq. President of the United States of America,
arrived in this city, with his suite, to the inexpressible
satisfaction as well of the citizens as of strangers. Never,
it may be truly said, was joy, love, affection, and esteem
more universal upon any one occasion—and never did
these amiable passions of the human heart, animate or
more brilliantly display themselves than upon this occasion—an occasion so worthy of their indulgence and
their operation.

Between 12 and 1 o'clock our amiable President embarked on board an elegant barge prepared for the purpose, and which anxiously waited his arrival at Hadrill's
Point, accompanied by Major Gen. Moultrie, Briga.
Gen. Pinckney, Major E. Rutledge, Col. Washington,
the City Recorder in his robes, Col. Dart, and Mr. John
Rutledge, jun. This illustriously freighted barge was
rowed across, Cooper River, from the place of embarkation to Charleston, by thirteen Masters of American vessels, viz. Capt. Cochran, (coxswain, as sen. officer) Captains Cross, Moore, Milligan, Kean, Rea,
Laurance, Drinker, Swain, Conyers, Dickenson,
Crowly, and Connelly, which last managed the bow
oar with peculiar adroitness: the gentlemen were uniformly and elegantly dressed in close short jackets of
light blue silk, black florentine breeches, with white
silk stockings, with light blue silk bow knots in their
shoes, rose wise; black round hats, with a light blue
wide sash round the crowns, bearing an elegant impres-

sion of the arms of this state, beneath which was this well adapted inscription,——"LONG LIVE THE PRESIDENT."

During the passage on the water, the gentlemen of the AMATEUR SOCIETY assisted by Mess. Palmer, James Badger, Jonathan Badger, and Harris, with their several choirs, performed a concert, as well vocal as instrumental, composed of pieces of music and choruses suited to the joyous occasion.——Among other select and much admired pieces, in the vocal strain, was sung, with peculiar harmony of numbers and skill of execution, the following:—

> He comes! he comes! the Hero comes!
> Sound, sound your trumpets, beat your drums.
> From port to port let cannons roar,
> He's welcome to our friendly shore.
>
> Prepare! prepare! your songs prepare!
> Loud, loudly read the echoing air;
> From pole to pole, his praise resound,
> For virtue is with glory crown'd.[1]

The grand coup d'oeil, exhibited by the presidental vehicle, which was distinguished from the rest by its ornaments, and the standard of the United States, which was displayed at the bow upon a ground of blue silk, accompanied by upwards of 40 rowing and sailing boats, filled every joyous, feeling breast ashore with sensations which we will not venture to describe, from a conviction of the impossibility of the task.

Stairs were erected at Prioleau's wharf, covered with green cloth, where the President was received on his landing by the Governor [Charles Pinckney], Lieutenant Governor [Isaac Holmes], and civil officers of the state; the Intendant and Wardens of the city, all dressed in black, carrying black staves headed with sil-

[1]See "Welcome to Newburyport," above.

ver, attended by their officers, with innumerable concourse of citizens, who welcomed our Chief Magistrate with reiterated shouts; the bells of St. Michael's church rang a joyful peal; the Charleston battalion of artillery fired a federal salute; and the fusileer company being drawn up at the landing, they opened their lines and inclosed the following order of procession, which moved with drums beating, colors flying, and fifes playing, towards the Exchange:[2]—

Sheriff of the city,
Messenger and Marshall,
Treasurer and Clerk,
Recorder,
Wardens,
Intendant,
PRESIDENT and SUIT,
Governor and Lieutenant Governor,
Aids to his Excellency the Governor,
Civil Officers of the State,
Civil Officers of the Union,
President of the Senate and Speaker of
the House of Representatives,
Clergy,
Citizens, two and two,

(The bakers particularly distinguished themselves by a rich blue flag, on which was represented various emblems of their occupation.)

Officers of the militia,
Members of the Cincinnati.

'Ere we proceed further we must observe, that there were such a concourse of all ranks on board of the several vessels hauled close to the shore, as is almost beyond all description. From superanuated old age to lisping infancy the croud was so great there was scarce

[2]The Exchange, an elegant customs house, was built in 1767–71 and served as Charleston's City Hall. After the state capitol burned on 5 February 1788, the legislature and the state ratifying convention met in the Exchange.

room to move!—On the illustrious personage's approach to the shore such a buz of approbation—such a
shout of joy took place as that one must have seen and
heard all to have any thing like an idea of it.——The
shores, the streets, the windows, the balconies—all were
so crouded, so beset with spectators, that the most at-
tentive observer must fail in an attempt to do justice
to the general ECLAT and splendid aspect of the whole.

Being arrived at the Exchange, the President was
conducted by the Governor, Lieutenant Governor, the
civil officers of the state already mentioned, and the
intendant and wardens of the city, to the platform before the ballustrade fronting Broad Street, where he
stood to await the salutes and discharges from the field
Artillery disposed for that purpose, as well as to see
the order of procession go by in review, when he returned all those salutations of respect which was rendered to him as it passed along.

The order of procession was then reversed, and
the President was escorted up Broad Street, while he
with the greatest politeness and attention bowed, uncovered, to the brilliant assemblage of spectators of
both sexes, to the right and to the left as he went along
(a conduct equally observed by him in the procession
from the landing place) till he arrived at the elegant
habitation destined for his reception in Church street,
which was ornamented in front, with lamps, festoons,
and over the portal, with a triumphal arch decorated
with laurels, flowers, &c. He there received the warm
congratulations of several of the most respectable characters in the state, and was individually introduced to
the members of the Cincinnati, and Officers of the
Charleston battalion of Artillery.

—*Virginia Herald*, 26 May 1791. Reprinted throughout
the country.

# "The Virtues and Talents of Soldier and Republican Statesman"

※ ※

*To the President of the United States.*

Sir, When, having accomplished the great objects of a war, marked in its progress with events that astonished while they instructed the world, you had again returned to the domestic enjoyments of life, to which you were known to be so strongly attached, there was little probability, in the common order of things, that the people of Georgia, however ardently they might desire, should ever be indulged the happiness of a personal interview with you—but summoned again, as you were, from your retirement, by the united voice and the obvious welfare of your country, you did not hesitate to furnish one more proof, that, in comparison to the great duties of social life, all objects of a private nature are with you but secondary considerations: And to this your ruling passion of love for your country it is that we owe the opportunity now afforded of congratulating you on your safe arrival in the city of Savannah—an office we the Committee, under the warmest impressions of sensibility and attachment, execute in the name and behalf of a respectable and grateful number of citizens.

History furnishes instances of some eminently qualified for the field, and of others endued with talents adequate to the intricate affairs of state; but you, Sir, have enriched the annals of America with a proof, to be sent abroad to mankind, that, however rare the association, the virtues and talents of soldier and republican stateman will some times dwell together, and both characters derive additional lustre from a subserviency to the precepts of religion.

Roused by oppression at home, and inspired by example from America, the people of enlightened nations in Europe are now beginning to assert their rights: and it is observable that those brave men, the subjects of foreign powers, who were votaries to our cause, and companions of your victories, are always found foremost in the struggle for just and equal government.

You have now, Sir, an opportunity of viewing a state which, from its exposed situation, has been peculiarly affected by the calamities of war, but which, under the influence of a happy government, will rise fast to that rank of prosperity and importance to which her natural advantages so justly entitle her, and which will enable her to reflect back upon the Union all the benefits derived from it.

We shall always take a deep concern, in common with the other citizens of the United States, in whatever regards your personal welfare and happiness. We make it our prayer to Almighty God, that you may be long continued to your country her Ornament and Father, and that it may be more and more exemplified in you, Sir, that to know how to conquer, and to improve the advantages of conquest into blessings to a community, are faculties some times bestowed on the same mortal.

In the name and behalf of a number of citizens of Savannah and its vicinity, convened for the reception of the President,

> N.W. Jones,
> Lach. M'Intosh,
> Joseph Clay,        } The Committee
> John Houstoun,
> Joseph Habersham,

*—Augusta Chronicle*, 4 June 1791. Also printed in the *Georgia Gazette*, 19 May 1791.

# A "Sensation Better Felt Than Expressed"

🦋 🦋

RICHARD VENABLE DIARY, 6–7 JUNE 1791

*Charlotte County, Virginia, Monday 6 June*
At Charlotte Court House. Great Anxiety in the people to see Gen'l. Washington. Strange is the impulse which is felt by almost every breast to see the face of a great good man—sensation better felt than expressed.

*Prince Edward County, Virginia, Tuesday, 7 June*
Gen'l. Washington arrived at Pr. Edward Court House, all crowding the way where they expect him to pass, anxious to see the saviour of their country and object of their love.

—Diary of Richard Venable, Virginia Historical Society. Venable was a twenty-eight year old lawyer from Prince Edward County, Va.

# V

## 🎔 🎔

# THE SECOND
# RETIREMENT

By 1792 President Washington looked forward longingly to his second retirement. He had succumbed to the overtures of his fellow Virginians to serve in the state delegation to the Constitutional Convention in 1787, and he had answered the call of the people to be President in 1789. But, now in 1792, the sixty-year-old President wanted to go home to Mount Vernon.

Washington's distaste for public office grew steadily during the early 1790s. What he had hoped would be a happy family turned into a quarrelsome Cabinet, while partisanship increased in Congress and throughout the country. Political struggles spilled over into the virulently partisan newspapers, sparing no one from their attacks. Despite all of Washington's efforts, he was unable to ameliorate the growing hostility between the Hamiltonians and the Jeffersonians. The President's distaste for the in-house bickering convinced him that it was time to retire.

In May 1792 Washington informed his closest advisors that he would not accept a second term as President. Hamilton, Jefferson, Madison, Knox and Edmund Randolph all begged him to reconsider. Retirement at this time would provoke crises both in domestic and foreign affairs. But Washington was immovable. He asked Madison to think about what was the best time to announce the retirement, whether a farewell address should be delivered, and what would be the best forum for such an address. On 20 June Madison delivered a draft address that he recommended be published in a newspaper in mid-September.

To a great extent Washington's advisors were correct—he was needed to solidify the institutions of the new government as well as to keep the country out of the worsening European maelstrom. Only three other men seemed to be viable presidential candidates in 1792—Vice President John Adams, Secretary of State Thomas Jefferson, and Chief Justice John Jay. Each of these men had strong support in his section of the country, but each was despised in other areas. Only Washington could command the respect and support of the entire country. Realizing that America was in fact entering a dangerous period, Washington resignedly agreed to be a candidate for a second term.

Four years later, Jefferson, Hamilton, Knox and Randolph—Washington's friends and advisors—were now all out of the Cabinet. Partisanship had mushroomed. Washington had become estranged from Jefferson and Madison, and the President was openly criticized in the Jeffersonian press. Washington made up his mind; he would not accept another term.

In May 1796 Washington sent a copy of Madison's draft farewell address to Hamilton, asking the former Treasury secretary either to revise it or write a new one. On 30 July Hamilton sent Washington a new draft, which included much from Madison's work. Hamilton told the President that he had tried "to render this act *importantly* and *lastingly* useful, . . . to embrace such reflections and sentiments as will wear well, progress in approbation with time, & redound to future reputation."

Washington decided to have his Address published in Philadelphia in *Claypoole's American Daily Advertiser*, from which, according to Hamilton, the Address would "of course find its way into all the other papers." The President gave the printer his manuscript copy of the Address. Proofs were made, checked and corrected; and the Address was published on 19 September 1796. Virtually every newspaper in the country reprinted it and many pamphlet editions were also published.

Washington hoped that the American people would accept his Address as the "disinterested warnings of a parting friend, who can possibly have no personal motive to biass his counsel." He advised Americans to cherish the Union—"a main Pillar in the Edifice of your real independence." The name "American," he said, "must always exalt the just pride of Patriotism" more than any feeling of localism. He warned against the dangers of sectionalism and described party spirit as "a fire not to be quenched; it demands a uniform vigilance to prevent its bursting into a flame, lest instead of warming it should consume." Washington recommended that his fellow citizens "avoid the necessity of those overgrown military establishments which . . . are inauspicious to liberty"; but he reminded Americans that military preparedness was absolutely necessary because "timely disbursements to prepare for danger frequently prevent much greater disbursements to repel it." He advised Americans to cherish public credit and avoid accumulating a public debt that would ungenerously throw "upon posterity the burthen which we ourselves ought to bear." Finally, he suggested an even-handed foreign policy without "permanent, inveterate antipathies against . . . or passionate attachments" to any individual countries. America should avoid permanent alliances, but enter into temporary pacts as needed. He ended his Address with the hope that his administration had been successful in giving America the chance "to settle and mature its yet recent institutions . . . to that degree of strength and consistency, which is necessary to give it, humanly speaking, the command of its own fortunes."

# An Inclination to Go Home

茇 茇

JAMES MADISON'S REPORT OF CONVERSATIONS
WITH GEORGE WASHINGTON

*5 May 1792*

In consequence of a note this morning from the
President requesting me to call on him I did so; when
he opened the conversation by observing that having
some time ago communicated to me his intention of
retiring from public life on the expiration of his four
years, he wished to advise with me on the *mode* and
*time* most proper for making known that intention. He
had he said spoken with no one yet on those particular
points, and took this opportunity of mentioning them
to me, that I might consider the matter, and give him
my opinion, before the adjournment of congress, or
my departure from Philadelphia. He had he said forborne to communicate his intention to any other persons whatever, but Mr. Jefferson, Col. Hamilton, General Knox & myself, and of late to Mr. Randolph. Col:
Hamilton & Genl. Knox he observed were extremely
importunate that he should relinquish his purpose, and
had made pressing representations to induce him to it.
Mr. Jefferson had expressed his wishes to the like effect.
He had not however persuaded himself that his continuance in public life could be of so much necessity
or importance as was conceived, and his disinclination
to it, was becoming every day more & more fixed; so
that he wished to make up his mind as soon as possible
on the points he had mentioned. What he desired was
to prefer that mode which would be most remote from
the appearance of arrogantly presuming on his re-elec-
tion in case he should not withdraw himself, and such
a time as would be most convenient to the public in

making the choice of his successor. It had, he said, at first occurred to him, that the commencement of the ensuing Session of Congress, would furnish him with an apt occasion for introducing the intimation, but besides the lateness of the day, he was apprehensive that it might possibly produce some notice in the reply of Congress that might entangle him in further explanations.

I replied that I would revolve the subject as he desired and communicate the result before my leaving Philada.; but that I could not but yet hope there would be no necessity at this time for his decision on the two points he had stated. I told him that when he did me the honor to mention the resolution he had taken, I had forborne to do more than briefly express my apprehensions that it would give a surprize and shock to the public mind, being restrained from enlarging on the subject by an unwillingness to express sentiments sufficiently known to him; or to urge objections to a determination, which if absolute, it might look like affectation to oppose; that the aspect which things had been latterly assuming, seemed however to impose the task on all who had the opportunity, of urging a continuance of his public services; and that under such an impression I held it a duty, not indeed to express my wishes which would be superfluous, but to offer my opinion that his retiring at the present juncture, might have effects that ought not to be hazarded; that I was not unaware of the urgency of his inclination; or of the peculiar motives he might feel to withdraw himself from a situation into which it was so well known to myself he had entered with a scrupulous reluctance; that I well recollected the embarrassments under which his mind labored in deciding the question, on which he had consulted me, whether it could be his duty to accept his present station after having taken a final leave of public life; and that it was particularly in my recollection, that I then entertained & intimated a wish that his acceptance, which appeared to be indispensable, might be known hereafter to have been in no degree the effect of any motive which strangers to his character might suppose. but of the severe sacrifice which his friends knew, he made of his inclinations as a man, to his obligations as a citizen; that I owned I had at that time contemplated, & I believed, suggested as the most unequivocal tho' not the only proof of his real motives, a voluntary return to private life as soon as the state of the Government would permit, trusting that if any premature casualty should unhappily cut off the possibility of this proof, the evidence known to his friends would in some way or other be saved from oblivion and do justice to his character; that I was not less anxious on the same point now than I was then; and if I did not conceive that reasons of a like kind to those which required him to undertake, still required him to retain from some time longer, his present station; or did not presume that the purity of his motives would be sufficiently vindicated, I should be the last of his friends to press, or even to wish such a determination.

He then entered on a more explicit disclosure of the state of his mind; observing that he could not believe or conceive himself anywise necessary to the successful administration of the Government; that on the contrary he had from the beginning found himself deficient in many of the essential qualifications, owing to his inexperience in the forms of public business, his unfitness to judge of legal questions, and questions arising out of the Constitution; that others more conversant in such matters would be better able to execute the trust; that he found himself also in the decline of life, his health becoming sensibly more infirm, & perhaps his faculties also; that the fatigues & disagreeableness of his situation were in fact scarcely tolerable to him; that he only uttered his real sentiments when he declared that his inclination would lead him rather to go to his farm, take his spade in his hand, and work for his bread, than remain in his present situation; that it was evident moreover that a spirit of party in the Government was becoming a fresh source of difficulty, and he was afraid was dividing some (alluding to the Secretary of State & Secry. of the Treasury) more particularly connected with him in the administration; that there were discontents among the people which were also shewing themselves more & more, & that altho' the various attacks against public men & measures had not in general been pointed at him, yet in some instances it had been visible that he was the indirect object, and it was probable the evidence would grow stronger and stronger that his return to private life was consistent with every public consideration, and consequently that he was justified in giving way to his inclination for it.

I was led by this explanation to remark to him, that however novel or difficult the business might have been to him, it could not be doubted that with the aid of the official opinions & informations within his command, his judgment must have been as competent in all cases, as that of any one who could have been put in his place, and in many cases certainly more so; that in the great point of conciliating and uniting all parties under a Govt. which had excited such violent controversies & divisions, it was well known that his services had been in a manner essential; that with respect to the spirit of party that was taking place under the operations of the Govt. I was sensible of its existence but considered that as an argument for his remaining, rather than retiring, until the public opinion, the character of the Govt. and the course of its administration shd. be better decided, which could not fail to happen in a short time, especially under his auspices; that the existing parties did not appear to be so formidable to the Govt as some had represented; that in one party there might be a few who retaining their original disaffection to the Govt. might still wish to destroy it, but that they would lose their weight with their associates, by betraying any such hostile purposes; that altho' it was pretty certain that the other were in general unfriendly to republican Govt. and probably aimed at a gradual approximation of ours to a mixt monarchy, yet the public sentiment was so strongly opposed to their views, and so rapidly manifesting itself, that the party could not long be expected to retain a dangerous influence; that it might reasonably be hoped therefore that the conciliating influence of a temperate & wise administration, would before another term of four years should run out, give such a tone & firmness to the Government as would secure it against danger from either of these descriptions of enemies; that altho' I would not allow myself to believe but that the Govt. would be safely administered by any successor elected by the peope, yet it was not to be denied that in the present unsettled condition of our young Government, it was to be feared that no successor would answer all the purposes to be expected from the continuance of the present chief magistrate; that the option evidently lay between a few characters; Mr. Adams, Mr. Jay & Mr Jefferson were most likely to be brought into view; that with respect to Mr Jefferson, his extreme repugnance to public life & anxiety to exchange it for his farm & his philosophy, made it doubtful with his friends whether it would be possible to obtain his own consent; and if obtained, whether local prejudices in the Northern States, with the views of Pennsylvania in relation to the seat of Govt. would not be a bar to his appointment.[1] With respect to Mr. Adams, his monarchical principles, which he had not concealed, with his late conduct on the

[1]In July 1790 Congress agreed to move the capital from New York City to Philadelphia beginning in December of that year. In 1800 the capital would be moved to a permanent site on the banks of the Potomac River. Philadelphians hoped that their city would remain the capital. A Jeffersonian presidency would guarantee the Southern site.

representation-bill had produced such a settled dislike among republicans every where & particularly in the Southern States, that he seemed to be out of the question.[2] It would not be in the power of those who might be friendly to his private character, & willing to trust him in a public one, notwithstanding his political principles, to make head against the torrent. With respect to Mr. Jay his election would be extremely dissatisfactory on several accounts. By many he was believed to entertain the same obnoxious principles with Mr. Adams, & at the same time would be less open and therefore more successful in propagating them. By others (a pretty numerous class) he was disliked & distrusted, as being thought to have espoused the claims of British Creditors at the expence of the reasonable pretensions of his fellow Citizens in debt to them. Among the western people, to whom his negociations for ceding the Mississippi to Spain were generally known, he was considered as their most dangerous enemy & held in peculiar distrust & disesteem.[3] In this state of our prospects, which was rendered more striking by a variety of temporary circumstances, I could not forbear thinking that altho' his retirement might

[2]Ever since he published his three-volume *Defence of the Constitutions of the United States* in 1787–88 while serving as U.S. minister to Great Britain, John Adams had been attacked, particularly in the South, as a friend of monarchy. His support for extravagant titles for the president increased the republican concern of many. Southern animosity to Adams heightened as a result of his tie-breaking vote in the Senate on the apportionment bill on 15 December 1791. The Senate bill lowered the ratio of representation from 1:30,000 to 1:33,000 and generally underrepresented the South in the House of Representatives.

[3]John Jay, Confederation Secretary for Foreign Affairs from 1784 to 1789, had been despised in the South and West ever since his negotiations for a Spanish-American treaty in 1786 became public. Jay had asked and received congressional permission to cede America's right to navigate the Mississippi River for twenty-five years in return for commercial concessions that benefitted the Northern States. No treaty was proposed.

not be fatal to the public good, yet a postponement of it was another sacrifice exacted by his patriotism.

Without appearing to be any wise satisfied with what I had urged, he turned the conversation to other subjects; & when I was withdrawing repeated his request that I would think of the points he had mentioned to me, & let him have my ideas on them before the adjournment. I told him I would do so: but still hoped his decision on the main question, would supersede for the present all such incidental questions.

*Wednesday Evening, 9 May 1792*

Understanding that the President was to set out the ensuing morning for Mount Vernon, I called on him to let him know that as far as I had formed an opinion of the subject he had mentioned to me, it was in favor of a direct address of notification to the public in time for its proper effect on the election, which I thought might be put into such a form as would avoid every appearance of presumption or indelicacy, and seemed to be absolutely required by his situation. I observed that no other mode deserving consideration had occurred, except the one he had thought of & rejected, which seemed to me liable to the objections that had weighed with him. I added that if on further reflection I shd. view the subject in any new lights, I would make it the subject of a letter tho' I retained my hopes that it would not yet be necessary for him to come to any opinion on it. He begged that I would do so, and also suggest any matters that might occur as proper to be included in what he might say to Congs. at the opening of their next Session; passing over the idea of his relinquishing his purpose of retiring, in a manner that did not indicate the slightest assent to it.

—Madison Papers, Library of Congress.

# Planning the Retirement Address

🐝 🐝

GEORGE WASHINGTON TO JAMES MADISON,
MOUNT VERNON, 20 MAY 1792

As there is a possibility if not a probability, that I shall not see you on your return home; or, if I should see you, that it may be on the Road and under circumstances which will prevent my speaking to you on the subject we last conversed upon; I take the liberty of committing to paper the following thoughts, & requests.

I have not been unmindful of the sentiments expressed by you in the conversations just alluded to: on the contrary I have again, and again revolved them, with thoughtful anxiety; but without being able to dispose my mind to a longer continuation in the Office I have now the honor to hold. I therefore still look forward to the fulfilment of my fondest and most ardent wishes to spend the remainder of my days (which I can not expect will be many) in ease & tranquility.

Nothing short of conviction that my deriliction of the Chair of Government (if it should be the desire of the people to continue me in it) would involve the Country in serious disputes respecting the chief Magestrate, & the disagreeable consequences which might result therefrom in the floating, & divided opinions which seem to prevail at present, could, in any wise, induce me to relinquish the determination I have formed: and of this I do not see how any evidence can be obtained previous to the Election. My vanity, I am sure, is not of that cast as to allow me to view the subject in this light.

Under these impressions then, permit me to reiterate the request I made to you at our last meeting— namely—to think of the proper time, and the best mode of anouncing the intention; and that you would prepare the latter. In revolving this subject myself, my judgment has always been embarrassed. On the one hand, a previous declaration to retire, not only carries with it the appearance of vanity & self importance, but it may be construed into a Manœuvre to be invited to remain. And on the other hand, to say nothing, implys consent; or, at any rate, would leave the matter in doubt; and to decline afterwards might be deemed as bad, & uncandid.

I would fain carry my request to you farther than is asked above, although I am sensible that your compliance with it must add to your trouble; but as the [congressional] recess may afford you leizure, and I flatter myself you have dispositions to oblige me, I will, without apology desire (if the measure in itself should strike you as proper, & likely to produce public good, or private honor) that you would turn your thoughts to a Valedictory address from me to the public; expressing in plain & modest terms—that having been honored with the Presidential Chair, and to the best of my abilities contributed to the Organization & Administration of the government—that having arrived at a period of life when the private Walks of it, in the shade of retirement, becomes necessary, and will be most pleasing to me; and the spirit of the government may render a rotation in the Elective Officers of it more congenial with their ideas of liberty & safety, that I take my leave of them as a public man; and in bidding them adieu (retaining no other concern than such as will arise from fervent wishes for the prosperity of my Country) I take the liberty at my departure from civil, as I formerly did at my military exit, to invoke a continuation of the blessings of Providence upon it—and upon all those who are the supporters of its interests, and the promoters of harmony, order & good government.

That to impress these things it might, among other things be observed, that we are *all* the Children of the same country—A country great & rich in itself—capable, & promising to be, as prosperous & as happy as any the Annals of history have ever brought to our view. That our interest, however diversified in local & smaller matters, is the same in all the great & essential concerns of the Nation. That the extent of our Country—the diversity of our climate & soil—and the various productions of the States consequent of both, are such as to make one part not only convenient, but perhaps indispensably necessary to the other part; and may render the whole (at no distant period) one of the most independant in the world. That the established government being the work of our own hands, with the seeds of amendment engrafted in the Constitution, may by wisdom, good dispositions, and mutual allowances; aided by experience, bring it as near to perfection as any human institution ever aproximated; and therefore, the only strife among us ought to be, who should be foremost in facilitating & finally accomplishing such great & desirable objects; by giving every possible support, & cement to the Union. That however necessary it may be to keep a watchful eye over public servants, & public measures, yet there ought to be limits to it; for suspicions unfounded, and jealousies too lively, are irritating to honest feelings; and oftentimes are productive of more evil than good.

To enumerate the various subjects which might be introduced into such an Address would require thought; and to mention them to you would be unnecessary, as your own judgment will comprehend *all* that will be proper; whether to touch, specifically, any of the exceptionable parts of the Constitu[t]ion may be doubted. All I shall add therefore at present, is, to beg the favor of you to consider—1st. the propriety of such an Address. 2d. if approved, the several matters which ought to be contained in it—and 3d. the time it should appear: that is, whether at the declaration of my intention to withdraw from the service of the public—or to let it be the closing Act of my Administration—which, will end with the next Session of Congress (the probability being that that body will continue sitting until March,) when the House of Representatives will also dissolve.

'Though I do not wish to hurry you (the cases not pressing) in the execution of either of the publications beforementioned, yet I should be glad to hear from you generally on both—and to receive them in time, if you should not come to Philadelphia until the Session commences, in the form they are finally to take. I beg leave to draw your attention also to such things as you shall conceive fit subjects for Communication on that occasion; and, noting them as they occur, that you would be so good as to furnish me with them in time to be prepared, and engrafted with others for the opening of the Session.

—Washington Papers, Pierpont Morgan Library, New York City. On his way from Mount Vernon back to Philadelphia, Washington met Madison and gave him this letter. Madison replied on 20 June (immediately below).

# "One More Sacrifice"

JAMES MADISON TO GEORGE WASHINGTON,
ORANGE, 20 JUNE 1792

Having been left to myself, for some days past, I have made use of the opportunity for bestowing on your letter of the 20 Ult: handed to me on the road, the attention which its important contents claimed. The questions which it presents for consideration, are 1. at what time a notification of your purpose to retire will be most convenient. 2 what mode will be most eligible. 3 whether a valedictory address will be proper and adviseable. 4 If both, whether it would be more properly annexed to the notification, or postponed to your actual retirement.

The answer to the 1st. question involves two points, first the expediency of delaying the notification; secondly the propriety of making it before the choice of electors takes place, that the people may make their choice with an eye to the circumstances under which the trust is to be executed. On the first point, the reasons for as much delay as possible are too obvious to need recital. The second, depending on the times fixed in the several States, which must be within thirty four days preceding the first wednesday in December, requires that the notification should be in time to pervade every part of the Union by the beginning of November. Allowing six weeks for this purpose, the middle of September or perhaps a little earlier, would seem a convenient date for the act.

2. With regard to the mode, none better occurs than a simple publication in the newspapers. If it were proper to address it through the medium of the general Legislature, there will be no opportunity. Nor does the change of situation seem to admit a recurrence to the State Governments which were the channels used for the former valedictory address. A direct address to the people who are your only constituents, can be made I think most properly through the independent channel of the press, through which they are, as a constituent body usually addressed.

3. On the third question I think there can be no doubt, that such an address is rendered *proper* in itself, by the peculiarity and importance of the circumstances which mark your situation; and *adviseable*, by the salutary and operative lessons of which it may be made the vehicle. The precedent at your military exit, might also subject

an omission now to conjectures and interpretations, which it would not be well to leave room for.

4. The remaining question is less easily decided. Advantages and objections lie on both sides of the alternative. The occasion on which you are *necessarily* addressing the people, evidently introduces most easily and most delicately any *voluntary* observations that are meditated. In another view a farewell address, before the final moment of departure, is liable to the appearance of being premature and awkward. On the opposite side of the alternative, however, a postponement will beget a dryness, and an abridgment in the first address, little corresponding with the feelings which the occasion would naturally produce both in the author and the objects; and though not liable to the above objection, would require a resumption of the subject apparently more forced; and on which, the impressions having been anticipated & familiarized, and the public mind diverted perhaps to other scenes, a second address would be received with less sensibility and effect, than if incorporated with the impressions incident to the original one. It is possible too, that previous to the close of the term, circumstances might intervene in relation to public affairs or the succession to the Presidency, which would be more embarrassing, if existing at the time of a valedictory appeal to the public, than if subsequent to that delicate measure.

On the whole my judgment leans to the propriety of blending together the notifying and valedictory address; and the more so as the crisis which will terminate your public career may still afford an opportunity, if any intermediate contingency should call for a supplement to your farewell observations. But as more correct views of the subject may produce a different result in your mind, I have endeavored to fit the draught inclosed to either determination. You will readily observe that in executing it I have aimed at that plainness & modesty of language which you had in view, and which indeed are so peculiarly becoming the character and the occasion; and that I have had little more to do, as to the matter, than to follow the just and comprehensive outline which you had sketched. I flatter myself however that in every thing which has depended on me, much improvement will be made, before so interesting a paper shall have taken its last form.

Having thus, Sir, complied with your wishes, by proceeding on a supposition that the idea of retiring from public life is to be carried into execution, I must now gratify my own by hoping that a reconsideration of the measure in all its circumstances and consequences, will have produced an acquiescence in one more sacrifice, severe as it may be, to the desires and interests of your country. I forbear to enter into the arguments which in my view plead for it; because it would be only repeating what I have already taken the liberty of fully explaining: But I could not conclude such a letter as the present without a repetition of my anxious wishes & hopes, that our country may not, in this important conjuncture, be deprived of the inestimable advantage of having you at the head of its councils.

—Robert A. Rutland and Thomas A. Mason, eds., *The Papers of James Madison*, Vol. 14 (Charlottesville, Va., 1983), 319–21. Madison enclosed a draft of a farewell address.

# "A Further Sacrifice"

⚒ ⚒

ALEXANDER HAMILTON TO GEORGE WASHINGTON,
PHILADELPHIA, 30 JULY 1792

I received the most sincere pleasure at finding in our last conversation, that there was some relaxation in the disposition you had before discovered to decline a re election. Since your departure, I have lost no opportunity of sounding the opinions of persons, whose opinions were worth knowing, on these two points. 1st the effect of your declining upon the public affairs, and upon your own reputation, 2dly the effect of your continuing, in reference to the declarations you have made of your disinclination to public life—And I can truly say, that I have not found the least difference of sentiment, on either point. The impression is uniform—that your declining would be to be deplored as the greatest evil, that could befall the country at the present juncture, and as critically hazardous to your own reputation—that your continuance will be justified in the mind of every friend to his country by the evident necessity for it. Tis clear, says every one, with whom I have conversed, that the affairs of the national government are not yet firmly established—that its enemies, generally speaking, are as inveterate as ever—that their enmity has been sharpened by its success and by all the resentments which flow from disapppointed predictions and mortified vanity—that a general and strenuous effort is making in every state to place the administration of it in the hand of its enemies, as if they were its safest guardians—that the period of the next house of representatives is likely to prove the crisis of its permanent character—that if you continue in office nothing materially mischievous is to be apprehended—

if you quit much is to be dreaded—that the same motives which induced you to accept originally ought to decide you to continue till matters have assumed a more determinate aspect—that indeed it would have been better, as it regards your own character, that you had never consented to come forward, than now to leave the business unfinished and in danger of being undone—that in the event of storms arising there would be an imputation either of want of foresight or want of firmness—and, in fine, that on public and personal accounts, on patriotic and prudential considerations, the clear path to be pursued by you will be again to obey the voice of your country; which it is not doubted will be as earnest and as unanimous as ever. . . .

I trust, Sir, and I pray God that you will determine to make a further sacrifice of your tranquillity and happiness to the public good. I trust that it need not continue above a year or two more—And I think that it will be more eligible to retire from office before the expiration of the term of an election, than to decline a re election.

The sentiments I have delivered upon this occasion, I can truly say, proceed exclusively from an anxious concern for the public welfare and an affectionate personal attachment . . .

—Washington Papers, Library of Congress.

# The Farewell

☙ ☙

*Friends, and Fellow-Citizens:*

The period for a new election of a Citizen, to Administer the Executive government of the United States, being not far distant, and the time actually arrived, when your thoughts must be employed in designating the person, who is to be cloathed with that important trust, it appears to me proper, especially as it may conduce to a more distinct expression of the public voice, that I should now apprise you of the resolution I have formed, to decline being considered among the number of those, out of whom a choice is to be made.—

I beg you, at the sametime, to do me the justice to be assured, that this resolution has not been taken, without a strict regard to all the considerations appertaining to the relation, which binds a dutiful citizen to his country—and that, in withdrawing the tender of service which silence in my situation might imply, I am influenced by no diminution of zeal for your future interest, no deficiency of grateful respect for your past kindness; but am supported by a full conviction that the step is compatible with both.

The acceptance of, & continuance hitherto in, the office to which your Suffrages have twice called me, have been a uniform sacrifice of inclination to the opinion of duty, and to a deference for what appeared to be your desire.—I constantly hoped, that it would have been much earlier in my power, consistently with motives, which I was not at liberty to disregard, to return to that retirement, from which I had been reluctantly drawn.—The strength of my inclination to do this, previous to the last Election, had even led to the preparation of an address to declare it to you; but mature reflection on the then perplexed & critical posture of our Affairs with foreign Nations, and the unanimous advice of persons entitled to my confidence, impelled me to abandon the idea.—

I rejoice, that the state of your concerns, external as well as internal, no longer renders the pursuit of inclination incompatible with the sentiment of duty, or propriety; & am persuaded whatever partiality may be retained for my services, that in the present circumstances of our country, you will not disapprove my determination to retire.—

The impressions, with which I first undertook the arduous trust, were explained on the proper occasion.— In the discharge of this trust, I will only say, that I have, with good intentions, contributed towards the Organization and Administration of the government, the best exertions of which a very fallible judgment was capable.—Not unconscious, in the outset, of the inferiority of my qualifications, experience in my own eyes, perhaps still more in the eyes of others, has strengthned the motives to diffidence of myself; and every day the encreasing weight of years admonishes me more and more, that the shade of retirement is as necessary to me as it will be welcome.—Satisfied that if any circumstances have given peculiar value to my services, they were temporary, I have the consolation to believe, that while choice and prudence invite me to quit the political scene, patriotism does not forbid it.—

In looking forward to the moment, which is intended to terminate the career of my public life, my feelings do not permit me to suspend the deep acknowledgment of that debt of gratitude wch. I owe to my beloved country,—for the many honors it has conferred upon me; still more for the stedfast confidence with which it has supported me; and for the opportunities I have thence enjoyed of manifesting my inviolable attachment, by services faithful & persevering, though in usefulness unequal to my zeal.—If benefits have resulted to our country from these services, let it always be remembered to your praise, and as an instructive example in our annals, that, under circumstances in which the Passions agitated in every direction were liable to mislead, amidst appearances sometimes dubious,—viscissitudes of fortune often discouraging,—in situations in which not unfrequently want of Success has countenanced the spirit of criticism, the constancy of your support was the essential prop of the efforts, and a guarantee of the plans by which they were effected.—Profoundly penetrated with this idea, I shall carry it with me to my grave, as a strong incitement to unceasing vows that Heaven may continue to you the choicest tokens of its beneficence— that your Union & brotherly affection may be perpetual—that the free constitution, which is the work of your hands, may be sacredly maintained—that its Administration in every department may be stamped with wisdom and Virtue—that, in fine, the happiness of the people of these States, under the auspices of liberty, may be made complete, by so careful a preservation and so prudent a use of this blessing as will acquire to them the glory of recommending it to the applause, the affection—and adoption of every nation which is yet a stranger to it.

Here, perhaps, I ought to stop. But a solicitude for your welfare, which cannot end but with my life, and the apprehension of danger, natural to that solicitude, urge me on an occasion like the present, to offer to your solemn contemplation, and to recommend to your frequent review, some sentiments; which are the result of much reflection, of no inconsiderable observation, and which appear to me all important to the permanency of your felicity as a People.—These will be offered to you with the more freedom, as you can only see in them the disinterested warnings of a parting friend, who can possibly have no personal motive to biass his counsel. Nor can I forget, as an encouragement to it, your endulgent reception of my sentiments on a former and not dissimilar occasion.

Interwoven as is the love of liberty with every ligament of your hearts, no recommendation of mine is necessary to fortify or confirm the Attachment.—

The Unity of Government which constitutes you one people is also now dear to you.—It is justly so;—for it is a Main Pillar in the Edifice of your real independence, the support of your tranquility at home; your peace abroad; of your safety;—of your prosperity;—of that very Liberty which you so highly prize.—But as it is easy to foresee, that from different causes & from different quarters, much pains will be taken, many artifices employed, to weaken in your minds the conviction of this truth; as this is the point in your political fortress against which the batteries of internal & external enemies will be most constantly and actively (though often covertly & insidiously) directed, it is of infinite moment, that you should properly estimate the immense value of your national Union to your collective & individual happiness;—that you should cherish a cordial, habitual & immoveable attachment to it; accustoming yourselves to think and speak of it as of the Palladium of your political safety and prosperity; watching for its preservation with jealous anxiety; discountenancing whatever may suggest even a suspicion that it can in any event be abandoned, and indignantly frowning upon the first dawning of every attempt to alienate any portion of our Country from the rest, or to enfeeble the sacred ties which now link together the various parts.—

For this you have every inducement of sympathy and interest.—Citizens by birth or choice, of a common country, that country has a right to concentrate your affections.—The name of AMERICAN, which belongs to you, in your national capacity, must always exalt the just pride of Patriotism, more than any appellation derived from local discriminations.—With slight shades of difference, you have the same Religion, Manners, Habits & political Principles.—You have in a common cause fought & triumphed together—The independence & liberty you possess are the work of joint councils, and joint efforts—of common dangers, sufferings and successes.—

But these considerations, however powerfully they address themselves to your sensibility are greatly outweighed by those which apply more immediately to your Interest.—Here every portion of our country finds the most commanding motives for carefully guarding & preserving the Union of the whole.

The *North*, in an unrestrained intercourse with the *South*, protected by the equal Laws of a common government, finds in the productions of the latter, great additional resources of Maratime & commercial enterprise and—precious materials of manufacturing industry.—The *South* in the same Intercourse, benefitting by the Agency of the *North*, sees its agriculture grow & its commerce expand. Turning partly into its own channels the seamen of the *North*, it finds its particular navigation envigorated;—and while it contributes, in different ways, to nourish & increase the general mass of the National navigation, it looks forward to the protection of a Maratime strength, to which itself is unequally adapted.—The *East*, in a like intercourse with the *West*, already finds, and in the progressive improvement of interior communications, by land & water, will more & more find a valuable vent for the commodities which it brings from abroad, or manufactures at home.—The *West* derives from the *East* supplies requisite to its growth & comfort, and what is perhaps of still greater consequence, it must of necessity owe the *secure* enjoyment of indispensable *outlets* for its own productions to the weight, influence, and the future Maritime strength of the Atlantic side of the Union, directed by an indissoluble community of Interest as *one Nation.*—Any other tenure by which the *West* can hold this essential advantage, whether derived from its own seperate strength, or from an apostate & unnatural connection with any foreign Power, must be intrinsically precarious.

While then every part of our country thus feels an immediate & particular Interest in Union, all the parts combined cannot fail to find in the united mass of means & efforts greater strength, greater resource, proportionably greater security from external danger, a less frequent interruption of their Peace by foreign Nations;—and, what is of inestimable value! they must derive from Union an exemption from those broils and Wars between themselves, which so frequently afflict neighbouring countries, not tied together by the same government; which their own rivalships alone would be sufficient to produce, but which opposite foreign alliances, attachments & intriegues would stimulate & imbitter.—Hence likewise they will avoid the necessity of those overgrown Military establishments, which under any form of Government are inauspicious to liberty, and which are to be regarded as particularly hostile to Republican Liberty: In this sense it is, that your Union ought to be considered as a main prop of your liberty, and that the love of the one ought to endear to you the preservation of the other.—

These considerations speak a persuasive language to every reflecting & virtuous mind, and exhibit the continuance of the UNION as a primary object of Patriotic desire.—Is there a doubt, whether a common government can embrace so large a sphere?—Let experience solve it.—To listen to mere speculation in such a case were criminal.—We are authorized to hope that a proper organization of the whole, with the auxiliary agency of governments for the respective Subdivisions, will afford a happy issue to the experiment.—'Tis well worth a fair and full experiment. With such powerful and obvious motives to Union, affecting all parts of our country, while experience shall not have demonstrated its impractibility, there will always be reason to distrust the patriotism of those, who in any quarter may endeavor to weaken its bands.—

In contemplating the causes wch. may disturb our Union, it occurs as matter of serious concern, that any ground should have been furnished for characterizing parties by *Geographical* discriminations—*Northern* and *Southern*—*Atlantic* and *Western*; whence designing men may endeavour to excite a belief that there is a real difference of local interests and views. One of the expedients of Party to acquire influence, within particular districts, is to misrepresent the opinions & aims of other Districts.—You cannot shield yourselves too much against the jealousies & heart burnings which spring from these misrepresentations.—They tend to render Alien to each other those who ought to be bound together by fraternal affection.—The Inhabitants of our Western country have lately had a useful lesson on this head.—They have seen, in the Negociation by the Executive, and in the unanimous ratification by the Senate, of the Treaty with Spain, and in the universal satisfaction at that event, thoughout the United States, a decisive proof how unfounded were the suspicions propagated among them of a policy in the General Government and in the Atlantic States unfriendly to their Interests in regard to the MISSISSIPPI—They have been witnesses to the formation of two Treaties, that with G: Britain and that with Spain, which secure to them every thing they could desire, in respect to our Foreign relations, towards confirming their prosperity.—Will it not be their wisdom to rely for the preservation of these advantages on the UNION by wch. they were procured?—Will they not henceforth be deaf to those advisers, if such there are, who would sever them from their Brethren and connect them with Aliens?—

To the efficacy and permanency of Your Union, a

Government for the whole is indispensable.—No Alliances however strict between the parts can be an adequate substitute.—They must inevitably experience the infractions & interruptions which all Alliances in all times have experienced.—Sensible of this momentous truth, you have improved upon your first essay, by the adoption of a Constitution of Government, better calculated than your former for an intimate Union, and for the efficacious management of your common concerns.—This government, the offspring of our own choice uninfluenced and unawed, adopted upon full investigation & mature deliberation, completely free in its principles, in the distribution of its powers, uniting security with energy, and containing within itself a provision for its own amendment, has a just claim to your confidence and your support.—Respect for its authority, compliance with its Laws, acquiescence in its measures, are duties enjoined by the fundamental maxims of true Liberty.—The basis of our political systems is the right of the people to make and to alter their Constitutions of Government.—But the Constitution which at any time exists, 'till changed by an explicit and authentic act of the whole People, is sacredly obligatory upon all.—The very idea of the power and the right of the People to establish Government presupposes the duty of every Individual to obey the established Government.

All obstructions to the execution of the Laws, all combinations and Associations, under whatever plausible character, with the real design to direct, controul counteract, or awe the regular deliberation and action of the Constituted authorities are distructive of this fundamental principle and of fatal tendency.—They serve to organize faction, to give it an artificial and extraordinary force—to put in the place of the delegated will of the Nation, the will of a party—often a small but artful and enterprizing minority of the Community— and, according to the alternate triumphs of different parties, to make the public administration the Mirror of the ill concerted and incongruous projects of faction, rather than the Organ of consistent and wholesome plans digested by common councils and modified by mutual interests.—However combinations or Associations of the above description may now & then answer popular ends, they are likely, in the course of time and things, to become potent engines, by which cunning, ambitious and unprincipled men will be enabled to subvert the Power of the People, & to usurp for themselves the Reins of Government; destroying afterwards the very engines which have lifted them to unjust dominion.—

Towards the preservation of your Government and the permanency of your present happy state, it is requisite, not only that you steadily discountenance irregular oppositions to its acknowledged authority, but also that you resist with care the spirit of innovation upon its principles however specious the pretexts.—one method of assault may be to effect, in the forms of the Constitution, alterations which will impair the energy of the system, and thus to undermine what cannot be directly overthrown.—In all the changes to which you may be invited, remember that time and habit are at least as necessary to fix the true character of Governments, as of other human institutions—that experience is the surest standard, by which to test the real tendency of the existing Constitution of a Country—that facility in changes upon the credit of mere hypotheses & opinion exposes to perpetual change, from the endless variety of hypotheses and opinion:—and remember, especially, that for the efficient management of your common interests, in a country so extensive as ours, a Government of as much vigour as is consistent with the perfect security of Liberty is indispensable—Liberty itself will find in such a Government, with powers properly distributed and adjusted, its surest Guardian.— It is indeed little else than a name, where the Government is too feeble to withstand the enterprises of faction, to confine each member of the Society within the limits prescribed by the laws & to maintain all in the secure & tranquil enjoyment of the rights of person & property.—

I have already intimated to you the danger of Parties in the State, with particular reference to the founding of them on Geographical discriminations.—Let me now take a more comprehensive view, & warn you in the most solemn manner against the baneful effects of the Spirit of Party, generally.

This spirit, unfortunately, is inseperable from our nature, having its root in the strongest passions of the human Mind.—It exists under different shapes in all Governments, more or less stifled, controuled, or repressed; but, in those of the popular form it is seen in its greatest rankness and is truly their worst enemy.—

The alternate domination of one faction over another, sharpened by the spirit of revenge natural to party dissention, which in different ages & countries has perpetrated the most horrid enormities, is itself a frightful despotism.—But this leads at length to a more formal and permanent despotism.—The disorders & miseries, which result, gradually incline the minds of men to seek security & repose in the absolute power of an Individual: and sooner or later the chief of some prevailing faction more able or more fortunate than his competitors, turns this disposition to the purposes of his own elevation, on the Ruins of Public Liberty.—

Without looking forward to an extremity of this kind (which nevertheless ought not to be entirely out of sight) the common & continual mischiefs of the spirit of Party are sufficient to make it the interest and the duty of a wise People to discourage and restrain it.—

It serves always to distract the Public Councils and enfeeble the Public Administration.—It agitates the Community with ill founded jealousies and false alarms, kindles the animosity of one part against another, foments occasionally riot & insurrection.—It opens the door to foreign influence & corruption, which find a facilitated access to the government itself through the channels of party passions. Thus the policy and the will of one country, are subjected to the policy and will of another.—

There is an opinion that parties in free countries are useful checks upon the Administration of the Government and serve to keep alive the Spirit of Liberty.—This within certain limits is probably true—and in Governments of a Monarchical cast Patriotism may look with endulgence, if not with favour, upon the spirit of party.—But in those of the popular character, in Governments purely elective, it is a spirit not to be encouraged.—From their natural tendency, it is certain there will always be enough of that spirit for every salutary purpose.—And there being constant danger of excess the effort ought to be, by force of public opinion, to mitigate & assuage it.—A fire not to be quenched; it demands a uniform vigilance to prevent its bursting into a flame, lest instead of warming it should consume.—

It is important, likewise, that the habits of thinking in a free Country should inspire caution in those entrusted with its administration, to confine themselves within their respective Constitutional spheres; avoiding in the exercise of the Powers of one department to encroach upon another.—The spirit of encroachment tends to consolidate the powers of all the departments in one, and thus to create whatever the form of government, a real despotism.—A just estimate of that love of power, and proneness to abuse it, which predominates in the human heart is sufficient to satisfy us of the truth of this position.—The necessity of Reciprocal checks in the exercise of political power; by dividing and distributing it into different depositories, & constituting each the Guardian of the Public Weal against invasions by the others, has been evinced by experiments ancient & modern;—some of them in our country & under our own eyes.—To preserve them must be as necessary as to institute them.—If in the opinion of the People, the distribution or modification of the Constitutional powers be in any particular wrong, let it be corrected by an amendment in the way which the Constitution designates.—But let there be no change by usurpation; for though this, in one instance, may be the instrument of good, it is the customary weapon by which free governments are destroyed.—The precedent must always greatly overbalance in permanent evil any partial or transient benefit which the use can at any time yield.—

Of all the dispositions and habits which lead to political prosperity, Religion and morality are indispensable supports.—In vain would that man claim the tribute of Patriotism, who should labour to subvert these great Pillars of human happiness, these firmest props of the duties of Men & citizens.—The mere Politician, equally with the pious man ought to respect & to cherish them.—A volume could not trace all their connections with private & public felicity.—Let it simply be asked where is the security for property, for reputation, for life, if the sense of religious obligation *desert* the oaths, which are the instruments of investigation in Courts of Justice?—And let us with caution indulge the supposition, that morality can be maintained without Religion.—Whatever may be conceded to the influence of refined education on minds of peculiar structure—reason & experience both forbid us to expect that National morality can prevail in exclusion of Religious principle.—

'Tis substantially true, that virtue or morality is a necessary spring of popular government.—The rule indeed extends with more or less force to every species of free Government.—Who that is a sincere friend to it, can look with indifference upon attempts to shake the foundation of the fabric.

Promote then as an object of primary importance, Institutions for the general diffusion of knowledge.— In proportion as the structure of a government gives force to public opinion, it is essential that public opinion should be enlightened.

As a very important source of strength & security, cherish public credit.—One method of preserving it is to use it as sparingly as possible:—avoiding occasions of expence by cultivating peace, but remembering also that timely disbursements to prepare for danger frequently prevent much greater disbursements to repel it—avoiding likewise the accumulation of debt, not only by shunning occasions of expence, but by vigorous exertions in time of Peace to discharge the Debts which unavoidable wars may have occasioned, not ungenerously throwing upon posterity the burthen which we ourselves ought to bear.—The execution of these maxims belongs to your Representatives, but it is necessary that public opinion should cooperate.—To facilitate to them the performance of their duty, it is essential that you should practically bear in mind, that towards the payment of debts there must be Revenue—that to have Revenue there must be taxes—that no taxes can be devised which are not more or less inconvenient & unpleasant—that the intrinsic embarrassment inseperable from the selection of the proper objects (which is always a choice of difficulties) ought to be a decisive motive for a candid construction of the Conduct of the Government in making it, and for a spirit of acquiescence in the measures for obtaining Revenue which the public exigencies may at any time dictate.—

Observe good faith & justice towds. all Nations. Cultivate peace & harmony with all—Religion & morality enjoin this conduct; and can it be that good policy does not equally enjoin it?—It will be worthy of a free, enlightened, and, at no distant period, a great Nation, to give to mankind the magnanimous and too novel example of a People always guided by an exalted justice & benevolence.—Who can doubt that in the course of time and things the fruits of such a plan would richly repay any temporary advantages wch. might be lost by a steady adherence to it? Can it be, that Providence has not connected the permanent felicity of a Nation with its virtue?—The experiment, at least, is recommended by every sentiment which ennobles human Nature.—Alas! is it rendered impossible by its vices?

In the execution of such a plan nothing is more essential than that permanent, inveterate antipathies against particular Nations and passionate attachments for others should be excluded; and that in place of them just & amicable feelings towards all should be cultivated.—The Nation, which indulges towards another an habitual hatred, or an habitual fondness, is in some degree a slave.—It is a slave to its animosity or to its affection, either of which is sufficient to lead it astray from its duty and its interest.—Antipathy in one Nation against another disposes each more readily to offer insult & injury, to lay hold of slight causes of umbrage, and to be haughty and intractable, when accidental or trifling occasions of dispute occur. Hence frequent collisions, obstinate envenomed and bloody contests. The Nation, prompted by ill will & resentment sometimes impels to War the Government, contrary to the best calculations of policy.—The Government sometimes participates in the national propensity, and adopts through passion what reason would reject;—at other times, it makes the animosity of the Nation subservient to projects of hostility instigated by pride, ambition and other sinister & pernicious motives.—The peace often, sometimes perhaps the Liberty, of Nations has been the victim.—

So likewise, a passionate attachment of one Nation for another produces a variety of evils.—Sympathy for the favourite nation, facilitating the illusion of an imaginary common interest, in cases where no real common interest exists, and infusing into one the enmities of the other, betrays the former into a participation in the quarrels & Wars of the latter, without adequate inducement or justification:—It leads also to concessions to the favourite Nation of priviledges denied to others, which is apt doubly to injure the Nation making the concessions—by unnecessarily parting with what ought to have been retained—& by exciting jealousy, ill will, and a disposition to retaliate, in the parties from whom eql. priviledges are withheld: And it gives to ambitious, corrupted, or deluded citizens (who devote themselves to the favourite Nation) facility to betray, or sacrifice the interests of their own country, without odium, sometimes even with popularity;—gilding with the appearances of a virtuous sense of obligation a commendable deference for public opinion, or a laudable zeal for public good, the base or foolish compliances of ambition, corruption or infatuation.—

As avenues to foreign influence in innumerable ways, such attachments are particularly alarming to the truly enlightened and independent Patriot.—How many opportunities do they afford to tamper with domestic factions, to practice the arts of seduction, to mislead public opinion, to influence or awe the public Councils!—Such an attachment of a small or weak, towards a great & powerful Nation, dooms the former to be the satellite of the latter.—

Against the insidious wiles of foreign influence, (I conjure you to believe me fellow citizens) the jealousy of a free people ought to be *constantly* awake; since history and experience prove that foreign influence is one of the most baneful foes of Republican Government.—But that jealousy to be useful must be impartial; else it becomes the instrument of the very influence to be avoided, instead of a defence against it.—Excessive partiality for one foreign nation and excessive dislike of another, cause those whom they actuate to see danger only on one side, and serve to veil and even second the arts of influence on the other.—Real Patriots, who may resist the intriegues of the favourite, are liable to become suspected and odious; while its tools and dupes usurp the applause & confidence of the people, to surrender their interests.—

The Great rule of conduct for us, in regard to foreign Nations is in extending our commercial relations to have with them as little *political* connection as possible.—So far as we have already formed engagements let them be fulfilled, with perfect good faith.— Here let us stop.

Europe has a set of primary interests, which to us have none, or a very remote Relation.—Hence she must be engaged in frequent controversies, the causes of which are essentially foreign to our concerns.—Hence therefore it must be unwise in us to implicate ourselves, by artificial ties, in the ordinary vicissitudes of her politics, or the ordinary combinations & collisions of her friendships, or enmities:—

Our detached & distant situation invites and enables us to pursue a different course.—If we remain one People, under an efficient government, the period is not far off, when we may defy material injury from external annoyance;—when we may take such an attitude as will cause the neutrality we may at any time resolve upon to be scrupulously respected;—when belligerent nations, under the impossibility of making acquisitions upon us, will not lightly hazard the giving us provocation;—when we may choose peace or war, as our interest guided by our Justice shall Counsel.—

Why forego the advantages of so peculiar a situation?—Why quit our own to stand upon foreign ground?—Why, by interweaving our destiny with that of any part of Europe, entangle our peace and prosperity in the toils of European Ambition, Rivalship, Interest, Humour or Caprice?—

'Tis our true policy to steer clear of permanent

Alliances, with any portion of the foreign world—So far, I mean, as we are now at liberty to do it, for let me not be understood as capable of patronising infidility to existing engagements (I hold the maxim no less applicable to public than to private affairs, that honesty is always the best policy).—I repeat it therefore, let those engagements be observed in their genuine Sense.—But in my opinion, it is unnecessary and would be unwise to extend them.—

Taking care always to keep ourselves, by suitable establishments, on a respectably defensive posture, we may safely trust to temporary alliances for extraordinary emergencies.—

Harmony, liberal intercourse with all Nations, are recommended by policy, humanity and interest.—But even our Commercial policy should hold an equal and impartial hand:—neither seeking nor granting exclusive favours or preferences;—consulting the natural course of things;—diffusing & deversifying by gentle means the streams of Commerce, but forcing nothing;—establishing with Powers so disposed—in order to give to trade a stable course, to define the rights of our Merchants, and to enable the Government to support them—conventional rules of intercourse; the best that present circumstances and mutual opinion will permit, but temporary, & liable to be from time to time abandoned or varied, as experience and circumstances shall dictate; constantly keeping in view, that 'tis folly in one Nation to look for disinterested favors from another—that it must pay with a portion of its Independence for whatever it may accept under that character—that by such acceptance, it may place itself in the condition of having given equivalents for nominal favours and yet of being reproached with ingratitude for not giving more.—There can be no greater error than to expect, or calculate upon real favours from Nation to Nation.—'Tis an illusion which experience must cure, which a just pride ought to discard.—

In offering to you, my Countrymen, these counsels of an old and affectionate friend, I dare not hope they will make the strong and lasting impression, I could wish—that they will controul the usual current of the passions, or prevent our Nation from running the course which has hitherto marked the Destiny of Nations:— But if I may even flatter myself, that they may be productive of some partial benefit, some occasional good;— that they may now & then recur to moderate the fury of party spirit, to warn against the mischiefs of foreign Intriegue, to guard against the Impostures of pretended patriotism—this hope will be a full recompence for the solicitude for your welfare, by which they have been dictated.—

How far in the discharge of my Official duties, I have been guided by the principles which have been delineated, the public Records and other evidences of my conduct must Witness to You and to the world.— To myself, the assurance of my own conscience is, that I have at least believed myself to be guided by them.

In relation to the still subsisting War in Europe, my Proclamation of the 22d. of April 1793 is the index to my Plan.[1]—Sanctioned by your approving voice and by that of Your Representatives in both Houses of Congress, the spirit of that measure has continually governed me;—uninfluenced by any attempts to deter or divert me from it.—

After deliberate examination with the aid of the best lights I could obtain I was well satisfied that our Country, under all the circumstances of the case, had a right to take, and was bound in duty and interest, to take a Neutral position.—Having taken it, I determined, as far as should depend upon me, to maintain it, with moderation, perseverence & firmness.—

[1]Washington's Neutrality Proclamation which declared the United States at peace with both Great Britain and France, and warning Americans against hostile actions against either belligerent.

The considerations, which respect the right to hold this conduct, it is not necessary on this occasion to detail.—I will only observe, that according to my understanding of the matter, that right, so far from being denied by any of the Belligerent Powers has been virtually admitted by all.—

The duty of holding a Neutral conduct may be inferred, without any thing more, from the obligation which justice and humanity impose on every Nation, in cases in which it is free to act, to maintain inviolate the Relations of Peace and amity towards other Nations.—

The inducements of interest for observing that conduct will best be referred to your own reflections & experience.—With me, a predominant motive has been to endeavour to gain time to our country to settle & mature its yet recent institutions, and to progress without interruption, to that degree of strength & consistency, which is necessary to give it, humanly speaking, the command of its own fortunes.—

Though in reviewing the incidents of my Administration, I am unconscious of intentional error—I am nevertheless too sensible of my defects not to think it probable that I may have committed many errors.—Whatever they may be I fervently beseech the Almighty to avert or mitigate the evils to which they may tend.—I shall also carry with me the hope that my Country will never cease to view them with indulgence; and that after forty five years of my life dedicated to its Service, with an upright zeal, the faults of incompetent abilities will be consigned to oblivion, as myself must soon be to the Mansions of rest.—

Relying on its kindness in this as in other things, and actuated by that fervent love towards it, which is so natural to a Man, who views in it the native soil of himself and his progenitors for several Generations;—I anticipate with pleasing expectation that retreat, in which I promise myself to realize, without alloy, the

sweet enjoyment of partaking, in the midst of my fellow Citizens, the benign influence of good Laws under
a free Government—the ever favourite object of my
heart, and the happy reward, as I trust, of our mutual
cares, labours, and dangers.

United States                                   Go. Washington
19th. September 1796

—New York Public Library.

# *Glory Augmented*

✠ ✠

James McHenry to George Washington,
Philadelphia, 25 September 1796

I thought it best to wait till I could ascertain the
full expression of the public sentiment, before I should
comply with your request, to tell you all, and conceal
nothing from you.

Your address on the first day of its publication, drew
from the friends of government, through every part of
the City, the strongest expressions of sensibility. I am
well assured, that many tears were shed on the occasion,
and propositions made in various companies, for so-
liciting your consent to serve another term; which were
afterwards dropped, on reflecting that nothing short of
a very solemn crises could possibly lead to a change of
your determination. The enemies of the government,
upon their part, discovered a sullenness, silence, and
uneasiness, that marked a considerable portion of cha-
green and alarm, at the impression which it was calculated to make on the public mind.

Such have been the *first effects* of an address which still continues to be a subject of melancholly conversation and regret. And I think I may safely add, that what has been exhibited here, will be found to be a transcript of the general expression of the people of the United States. I sincerely believe, that no nation ever felt a more ardent attachment to its chief; and 'tis certain, that history cannot furnish an example such as you have given. Those men who have relinquished sovereign power, have done it under circumstances which tarnished more or less the glory of the act; but in the present case, there is no circumstance which does not serve to augment it.

—Washington Papers, Library of Congress.

# INDEX

In this index, "George Washington" is abbreviated "GW." Several main entries are compilations of similar items: "Biblical References," "Classical Antiquities," "Music," and "Processions." All titles of documents are grouped under the entry "Document Titles," while page numbers for all poems are listed under the entry "Poetry." Two somewhat unusual entries are "Fame" and "God." Finally, the subentry "—appellations for" under the main entry "George Washington" lists all the names which Washington was called in the documents in this volume.